DOES CHRIST MATTER?

AN ANGLICAN AND A JESUIT IN DIALOGUE

TIMOTHY KINAHAN & BRIAN LENNON SJ

First published in 2017 by Messenger Publications

ISBN 978 1 910248 42 3

Designed by Messenger Publications Design Department
Typeset in Baskerville
Printed by Johnwood Press Limited

Messenger Publications,
37 Lower Leeson Street, Dublin D02 W938
www.messenger.ie

TABLE OF CONTENTS

SECTION 2: CRITIQUE OF CHURCHES

SECTION 3: CHURCH AND SOCIETY

Introduction

Does Christ matter?

If so, why?

If he does, how could one communicate this in today's culture?

What impact should – or could – Christians have on social and political issues?

These are big questions. Perhaps also surprising ones given that it is we who are asking them.

We are two priests:

Tim Kinahan, a Church of Ireland (Anglican) rector, and Brian Lennon, a Jesuit. These questions are real for us because we are on a journey. Indeed we have been on this journey since we were born, and we reckon it will continue for eternity.

Part of our journey has been made together, on and off over the past forty years. Our journey's context has been the divided society of Northern Ireland. We each live within different parts of the Northern Ireland community. This has meant that we have been immersed each within our own section of the community, understanding people's grievances and supporting their struggles to overcome them. Yet, it has also meant coming to understand the other side, by putting ourselves in their shoes, building relationships with them and communicating their world view within our own communities.

Our friendship with each other has been important to us for its own sake, but also because it has helped us to see beyond our own immediate world. We realise, as two people trying to follow Christ, that Christ wants his followers to be united. In part this is because he knows the pain division caused his Father. In part it is because Christian divisions are a scandal: they make the message of Christ less credible.

Our thinking, our living has been forged in the context of 'The Troubles' – as the terribly destructive conflict in Northern Ireland is known locally. This context has, for us, been both potent and creative despite manifest pains and frustrations. We have also been influenced by our experience of the wider world: the Republic of Ireland (from where Brian comes), England (where Tim went to school), Papua New Guinea and Ethiopia, which Tim visits frequently, and various works and projects in which we have been involved in Serbia, Moldova, S. Africa, Liberia, Cyprus, Malta and the USA.

Our reflections, then, come from our local base, but we have been greatly enriched by what we have learned from the people of other countries.

Does Christ matter? The answer for us is yes: we have given our lives to following him, however much we make a mess of that commitment. Christ matters to us because he can help us make sense of life, of who we are and what purpose our lives might serve. We can look at Christ Jesus, as presented to us in the New Testament, and as interpreted for us throughout the centuries, and find in him the key to a deeper understanding of life. Justin Martyr, one of the earliest Christian writers outside the pages of Scripture, spoke of the cruciform *Logos* ('Word of God') as the key to the universe. His message is as critical and alive today as it ever was.

The Word became flesh and dwelt among us *(Jn.1:14)*, revealing to all generations what God is, and always has been, like. He showed us God as one who refuses to dominate, who comes alongside, who listens.

To his first followers there was something about Jesus that was mind blowing. And there is something about him that is still mind blowing today.

Yet the 'yes' that we give to the question includes a large measure of doubt and struggle. We live in a Western world that has its measure of secularism. We are not immune to its influence.

Some time ago each of us was asked to write down what Christ meant to us. Brian wrote:

I have been 'caught' by Christ since a young age, despite various repeated efforts at avoiding him. The reason that avoidance failed was because the attraction in the end was always too strong: it always drew me back.

I find Christ in personal prayer, in the sacraments, in other people and in the world at large. Personal prayer remains something that operates at very different levels: noisy distractions and momentary silences. The latter, however, are worth anything and it is these that draw me back to prayer.

I also find God when I am with people who are suffering, perhaps especially as they face into death, and their loved ones know they are going to lose them. In a strange way I find my doubts silenced, at least temporarily. Somehow it seems to be a place where God is most present.

Also, when I think of people I know who are now dead, but who seem to me to be examples of great human living, I find that it is not sensible to believe that they have simply ceased to exist. There was too much life in them for nothingness to triumph.

The Faith and Politics Group, in which Tim and I were both members, and which we will discuss later, helped me build lasting relationships with people in other Christian communities, exposed me to new thinking and deepened my theology, especially in respect of the Eucharist.

The Eucharist has been central to me since I was a child. In it we are caught up in the sacrifice of Christ, in which he gave himself to his Father on the cross. In the Eucharist we are made part of his self-giving. This act of Christ was the final way in which he was reunited with his Father and the Holy Spirit.

The cross was not only about Christ returning to his Father. Christ died for all people, that all might be brought into communion with the Father. On the cross, then, Christ not only gave himself to the Father, he also brought all human beings with him on the journey. We are thereby made part of the life of the Trinity. That makes the Eucharist important.

The awkward part of this is that the rest of the world is involved since it is all the people of the world and not only ourselves that Christ brings to the Father in the Eucharist. The reason is simple: God loves all people. The social implications of this have always been obvious to me: we are called to create a world in which we live with all others on a journey to the inner life of the three divine persons.

This means a lot more than charity: people deserve justice because they are human, because they are images of God, and because they are made part of the three divine persons by Christ. So we need structures that are just. But we also need the respect and compassion of Christ.

Christ's incarnation is central to me. It means that God is to be found here, in our world, rather than in some distant heaven. So I will not find God in some mystical world in the skies. I will find God in the messiness of my life and relationships.

We are called to help the Kingdom of God to grow, here and now, despite all the corruption in the world and in ourselves. God is with us in this work and inspires us through the love of Christ. In his own life Christ showed us how to live life fully, truthfully and with love. The resurrection is the promise that in the end, despite all the negativity in ourselves and in the world, Christ's love will triumph.

The death of Christ shows also the vulnerability and powerlessness of God as well as the compassion of Christ. His forgiveness heals our brokenness. None of us therefore can be self-righteous without being foolish.

All of us can hope to see God face to face. But the anger of God is still real, precisely because God is a lover: as a lover God abhors God's loved ones being hurt. This anger, unlike ours, is never destructive, but is always a call to new life.

And then Tim:

'The Jesus event' is meaningless to me, as a child of the individualistic Enlightenment, if it is not primarily experienced at a personal level. It is from that personal experience, however defined, that all else flows.

For me the birth, death and resurrection of Jesus reveal the vulnerability of God. God becomes human and reveals to us thereby that his omnipotence is shown most completely in self-emptying (*Phil.2:7*). It is not for nothing that, outside the Book of Revelation and quotations from the Old Testament, the New Testament never once refers to God as 'almighty'. God comes alongside me, in my weakness and hurt, not to condemn, but to encourage.

The word of God becomes flesh; the impersonal becomes personal and the precision of the word becomes the enigma of a human being. Jesus reveals to me the humanity of God, in whose image we are made (*Gen.1:28*); he reveals a God who understands, from personal experience, what it is like to live here on earth, who knew the rough-and-tumble of family life, as well as tears and the pain of betrayal. He also knew of simple joys. God is not remote and distant like some immutable and apathetic monad but someone who can help because he has been where we are.

Jesus on the cross speaks to me of this divine vulnerability taken to extremes. The cross reveals that 'greater love' (*Jn.15:13*) which will stop at nothing for the beloved – me. It reveals also the welcome of God who, with arms outstretched, says 'come to me, all you who labour and are heavy-laden' (*Mt.11:28*). Somehow, on the cross, God is saying 'sorry'. Apologising, in some way, for this wonderful world not being the limitless joy that he had intended.

This 'Jesus event' conceptualises for me what I experience – God is somehow 'in me'. Awe-inspiring and majestic, but also intimate, patient and understanding. The story of Jesus makes sense of my experience of daily life and of my indescribable interaction with someone beyond myself. The story of Jesus challenges me to live, as he lived, beyond myself.

Not surprisingly, our belief in God comes with problems. We live and are immersed in a Northern European culture, with all its limitations. We are affected by it. So there are many days when we ask ourselves if God exists. Is our faith not simply wish-fulfilment? We want there to be an after-life, so do we not simply make it up? Are the secularists not correct? After all, neither of us has ever heard a corpse tell us anything about the next life. Doubts are part of our faith. One source of these doubts is false images of God.

Both of us struggle with images of God. We have inherited images: the wise old man in the sky; personal images, in which we sculpt a god to fit our own needs; communal images which confirm our prejudices and those of 'our' side when the going gets rough. Indeed one of the key foci of our ministry has been getting people (including ourselves) to let go of the God we thought we had: if that God exists then neither of us are interested in him – and it is nearly always a 'he'. These, despite some elements of truth, are imperfect images of God, and they are all around us, deeply embedded within our culture, within our Churches and within ourselves.

In the pages that follow we reflect on the images of God that we and others have. We look at what we see as crucially important values shown by Christ in the Scriptures. In the light of those values we critique our own Churches that are called to be signs of the presence of God. We do this as committed members, not as outsiders, and we are aware that we are often part of the problems we critique. Finally, we ask how we are called as followers of Christ to respond to political and social issues, including conflict.

Our reflection is based first on our experience of ministry for the past forty years, for the most part in a divided community. Secondly, it is based on what we have learned from one another through our dialogue, and also what we have learned from other traditions. This book, then, is an attempt at *praxis*. We understand *praxis* as the interface through which theology is tested by the furnace of experience, and in its turn experience is challenged by abstract thought. In that interface *both* the experience and the theory are important.

SECTION 1: WHAT IS GOD LIKE?

Chapter 1: Images of God

Secularism

Our world is deeply affected by secularism. According to secularism the world is the visible. God is not visible. So there is no God. Our world is also deeply infected by *scientism*. *Scientism* takes the marvels of the scientific method, which has achieved such wondrous outcomes in areas like that of medicine, and then draws conclusions that go beyond the scope of that method. We can explain the evolution of the world from the Big Bang, but not the origin of the elements that made up the Big Bang. In the past religions foolishly fought against scientific evidence and they were wrong to do so, but some now argue that science not only explains *how* something happens – which it does up to a point – but also *why* it happens.

This is a move towards interpreting *meaning*. The scientific method cannot do this. It can tell us neither *why* things happen nor what they mean. In teasing out the question 'Does Christ matter?' we will come back to the issue of secularism.

Bland God

A second theme that can make faith difficult – as well as strengthening it – is a tendency to make God into a bland, cardboard figure. The sources of this making-bland are sometimes important ideas, with positive content. An example is ecumenism.

At the root of ecumenism is the insight that God in Christ works beyond the boundaries of our Churches and cultures. That is a belief we hold dear: each of us has been strengthened in our faith and theology through what we have learnt from other traditions. Ecumenism, however, has always to wrestle with the danger of relativism. In many cases the charge of relativism is simply a cry of insecurity: we want the world to be simple and clear, and accepting the idea that other Churches and faiths have value can muddy the waters. We comment frequently in the pages that follow on the dangers of a religion based on insecurity. Yet, there is one important danger that ecumenists need to address: making God bland.

A second example is the idea that 'we all believe the same thing'. We don't. As it happens, we agree on most things, but there are some things about which we still disagree, as we will see when we come to critique our respective Churches. Further, while theologians have overcome almost all the issues that in the past divided our two Churches, we remain divided in the area of practice. As well as this there are obviously serious issues dividing different faiths. A danger in the admirable emphasis on respecting difference is to conclude – wrongly – that difference does not matter.

A third source is a misunderstanding of God's mercy. Showing that God is merciful is one of the most important tasks for all Christians, which is why Pope Francis made it a theme for a whole year, starting in December 2015. It is a vital balance to the god of terror who in the past threatened so many people with eternal damnation, often for doing things that we might now see as good, such as having independent thoughts. It is also currently present in some modern evangelical hymns, for example 'In Christ Alone'.

There is a danger, however, in seeing God as all merciful: making light of sin. If God is all merciful, then it is all too easy to slip into the delusion that it does not matter what wrongs we commit: God will forgive us, so hurting others does not matter that much. That attitude takes God's mercy for granted. It forgets the terrible price of God's love. It ignores the infinite pain that hurting others causes God.

Tie in with this false notion of God's mercy the idea that God can no longer perform miracles, and it is then easy to see God as a sort of irrelevant being in the sky.

Finally, we recognise that questions about God cannot be answered without diminishing God since ultimately God is a mystery. In that case what is the point of even discussing God?

For us God is anything but bland. We might be sympathetic to Karl Rahner's thought that Christ moves in other faiths, making their faithful into 'anonymous Christians', but for many this can be both patronising and simplistic. We are also aware that the Church's record in its relationships with people of other faiths (and variations of the Christian faith) has been far from edifying. Yet, we do not flinch from saying that Jesus is decisive, not just for us, but for all of history. He is of ultimate importance for all people, not least for us in Ireland today. What he says and who he is transcends our inherited divisions, as we hope our common enterprise in writing this book makes clear.

What did Christ try to do in his life? What was his dream? How did he attempt to turn that dream into reality? How did he cope with failure? One important source for answering these questions is the Scriptures, and we now want to look at some of the answers they suggest.

Chapter 2: What Sort of Community Did Jesus Want?

We have spent a good deal of our adult lives trying to make sense of the story of Christ in the Scriptures. Making sense of it means trying to see how it connects to our lives today, and working out what we are called to do because of our relationship with Christ. What does that mean? What do the Scriptures tell us about Christ's life and about what mattered most to him? There is a world of answers to these questions. They can be responded to at a general level, but in the gospels Christ, after asking 'Who do men say that I am?', asks a different question of Peter: 'Whom do you say that I am?' (*Mk. 8:20*). The answer to that question lies in what we emphasise in the Scriptures, in our theology, in our values, our relationships and ultimately in what matters most to us in life.

In this section we answer the question for ourselves: what do we think are the most striking parts of Scripture about Christ's life? We hope that in doing so we can pose the question helpfully for others as well, because we remain convinced that this question is the most important one in the world. In the sections that follow we will tease out the implications. In doing this we are not simplistically assuming that today we need to do everything as Christ did. Our world, our understanding, our contexts are different. Our question, therefore, is: given the values that we see in Our Lord, in what way are we called to apply them in our very different world of today? The question is important: if Christ is at the centre of our lives, then acting in a way that is in accordance with the mind of Christ is vital.

The covenant community

Jesus was Jewish. As such he was immersed in his people's Scriptures, what we call the Old Testament. In this, God makes a covenant or agreement with his chosen people: God will free the people from oppression, bring them to a land flowing with milk and honey, and will always remain faithful to them. For their part the people are asked to respond by loving God and loving their neighbour. The principal way they will do this is by obeying God's law, which is given to them as their guide in the covenant.

In practice the people break the covenant in two ways: by idolatry, and by social injustice, both of which alienate them from God. In idolatry the people put things before the God of all creation. By acting unjustly they violate the sanctity of fellow human beings who are also made in the image of God. Social injustice makes worship a sham (a 'trampling of my courts' (*Isa. 1:12*). God does not require sacrifice, but mercy (*Hos. 6:6*): 'He has showed you, O man, what is good; and what does the Lord require of you but to do justice, to love kindness and to walk humbly with your God?' (*Mic. 6:8*). Meeting God in true worship requires entering into a new relationship with all our brothers and sisters. Without this the covenant is broken.

The story of the New Testament is of a small group of Jewish people discovering one of their own, Christ, as the new covenant, the new agreement between God and humankind. In Jesus, the old impersonal covenant with a sometimes impersonal God became a personal intervention into current reality. As with the old covenant, compassion is at the centre of the new covenant, above all for the excluded and marginalised.

The Kingdom of God

The Kingdom of God was at the very centre of Christ's teaching in the New Testament. The Kingdom is the new society of respect, forgiveness and justice that Our Lord came to inaugurate. It is not only for the chosen people, but for the many who will come from 'the East and the West' (*Mt.8:11*). People join the community of the Kingdom by repenting and turning away from sin, by finding and showing forgiveness. 'Forgive us our trespasses as we forgive those who trespass against us'. The Kingdom is really the upside-down world of the Beatitudes where the poor, those who mourn and those who hunger and thirst for justice are blessed. It is the new society where barriers and divisions, like those between the Jews and Samaritans, or between the Pharisees and the tax collectors, are broken down. It is not only a spiritual kingdom but one in which all our relationships are based on respect in the concrete here and now. The Kingdom of God is realised wherever these values are lived.

Christ himself is the perfect example of the kingdom person. In him fear, enmity and domination are broken down: fear is faced and overcome in the Garden of Gethsemane (*Mt.26:36-46*), enmity is overcome on the cross as he prays 'Father, forgive them for they know not what they do' (*Lk.23:34*), and domination is overcome by the life of him 'who came to serve and not to rule' (*Lk.22:27*). 'The defeat of the cross, the apparent victory of Christ's enemies, is in fact the triumph of love, the overpowering of the forces of evil, the redemption of the world'[1]

Idolatry

Idolatry was one of the ways in which the chosen people of Israel rejected God. 'Worshipping idols' is not just a quaint, pictorial Old Testament phrase, now obsolete. It refers to something real in every society, including our own; it is regarding something as more important than love of God and love of our neighbour. The Old Testament emphasises that all peoples within the covenant community, including those who had been pushed to its margins – the widows, the orphans, the strangers – have the right to be treated with dignity. The degree of idolatry in society can be measured by the extent to which marginalised people are respected. In other words, idolatry and injustice are different aspects of the same problem, an equation that was central to the message of the Prophets of the eighth century BC – Isaiah, Amos, Hosea and Micah.

Idolatry is toxic because it dehumanises us. It offers an illusion of freedom in which we think that we are 'free' from God, the source of true humanity. Idolatry (and its close relative greed) says that inanimate things such as wealth and ideals are of more value than relationships and people. Therefore, idolatry stultifies and deforms. It is destructive.

Sin

'Sin' is a small word with a big history. It is also a word rarely used outside a church context. Many Christians seem too embarrassed even to mention it, perhaps from the fear of appearing judgmental or self-righteous. As a result, the concept of 'sin' has also lost much of its past emphasis. Many things seen as sinful by our forebears are accepted as moral today.

Behind this lies a new belief: many claim that the choices of individuals are seen as their private concern, so long as they do not adversely affect others.

The pendulum can swing with bewildering speed. Attitudes to homosexuality, euthanasia and divorce among others, have changed incredibly fast in recent years, particularly in the West.

Theologians and preachers have conventionally thought of sin as something that comes between us and God and which hinders our full development as human beings. It is much more than this, however. Because of the incarnation, theology and anthropology coincide: the way that we treat other people is the way we treat God; the way that we think of other people is the way we think of God. So, if we create unreasonable barriers between people we sin; if we hurt others unreasonably, we sin; if we stop others unreasonably achieving their full potential we sin. When we sin we separate ourselves to a greater or lesser extent from the Kingdom of God. Therefore we need to turn away from our sins, repent and seek the forgiveness of God and of those we have hurt.

Sin is also more, much more, than acts by individuals that separate them from each other, and from God. Sin is *social*: our sins in some sense are cumulative. We are born into a world in which our ancestors have sinned. We make our own contribution to this cumulative sin. So, while human beings are intrinsically good, because we are born in the image of God, and because we have been redeemed by Christ, we are also part of a fallen world. This, in a very inadequate way, touches on the bondage of sin, about which St Paul speaks (*Rom. 7:14*).

Temptations

The story of the temptations occurs in all three synoptic gospels (Matthew, Mark and Luke). Because of this, and also because it is not the kind of story the disciples would have told if they could have avoided doing so, it is likely that the fact of the temptations has an historical basis. Further, other gospel texts suggest that throughout his life Jesus was tempted to respond in ways that he gradually saw were not in accordance with the Father's will.

One of the temptations was to turn stone into bread. Why not do so? People were hungry: there was no social welfare, and the Romans and tax collectors ensured that people often had no money for food. Today the cries of the hungry around the world would scream at Our

Lord to do it. Obviously he was tempted to do so: that is what the story is about. Yet, in the end he refused. Instead he chose a path of powerlessness, one in which he would not impose an answer on us. God, in Christ, handed power over to us. During the temptations Christ chose to affirm this decision.

In doing so Christ avoided one outcome: were God a magician, then there would be no need for us to respond as humans. We could simply lie back and God would sort out all our problems. Our capacity to grow as human beings would be gone. So too would our responsibility for each other. The fact that children are dying painfully and needlessly as you read this would not be a real problem because God would sort it. In refusing the temptations Christ chose to treat us instead as humans: God left us the power to respond or not. Thereby God gave us the opportunity to become lovers instead of robots, responsible adults instead of machines.

Diversity

It seems that Jesus did not take easily to diversity. His focus initially was on his own Jewish people, but gradually he was challenged to reach beyond this. Hints of this can be seen in the stories of the healing of the centurion's servant (*Mt. 8:5-13*), the woman at the well in Samaria (*Jn. 4*), the Greeks to whom Phillip introduced him (*Jn. 12:20-22*), and the healing of the daughter of the Canaanite woman (*Mt. 15*).

In the early church, the first experience that the disciples had of the Holy Spirit at Pentecost was one of diversity: people from different nations heard the disciples speak in their own language.

In the gospel texts it is often not possible to distinguish Jesus' own words from those of the early church members who were initially all Jewish and who were put out of their synagogues by their Jewish compatriots who rejected Christ. That led to bitter struggles and feelings, and to the great battle between Paul on the one hand and the

Jerusalem church led by James and Peter on the other as to whether they should accept Gentiles into their community and, if so, under what terms.

It is difficult for us to have any real idea of the shocking struggle to which this led. The law was at the centre of Jewish identity. According to that law Jewish men had to be circumcised and be bound by dietary rules. Paul rejected this aspect of the law. For many Jewish people of his time that meant rejecting what it meant to be Jewish. Yet, Paul was unrelenting. He did not reject the Jewish law: in Phil 3:6 he claimed to be blameless under the law. Yet, he did reject a central statement about the law: human beings could not be saved by it they could only be saved by Christ, and not through any merit or action of their own but through the gracious love of God in Christ. Because Paul won that battle, those of us who are not Jewish have been able to take our place in the community of Church. We therefore have a model in our history of how to respond to the stranger.

In all this Jesus showed himself willing to be confronted by people from whom he differed, and to engage with them.

The outcome of these struggles was that diversity became central to the Church of Christ. The Church, to which both of our denominations belong, is 'Catholic' or universal. Without this it lacks an important element of Christ's church.

Justice and peace

Christ was passionate about justice. The reason for this is simple: Christ in his own person is the incarnation of the God of loving kindness and justice and he sees all people as his brothers and sisters. So he wants us to be happy, to live life to the full. Being fully human includes treating people with respect. So Christ is disappointed with us when we fail to do this because we harm his family, and we harm ourselves.

At the root of the gospel disputes between Christ and the Pharisees was his anger at their injustice.

'They tie up heavy burdens and lay them on people's shoulders, but will they lift a finger to move them? Not they!' (*Mt.23:4*).

In doing this, they

> 'shut up the kingdom of Heaven in people's faces, neither going in yourselves nor allowing others to go who want to.' (*Mt.23:13,14*).

They are

> 'like whitewashed tombs that look handsome on the outside, but inside are full of dead men's bones and every kind of corruption…a brood of vipers' (*Mt.23:27*).

Jesus himself may have been a Pharisee, but whether he was or not he challenged the leaders of his own people, and did so in a very confrontational way. There was nothing meek or mild about it. These passages also reflect the battles between the Jewish people who followed Christ and their brothers and sisters who not only rejected Christ but expelled his followers from the synagogue. They are part of the struggle that led to the tragic split between Jews and Christians: a struggle between the law that was at the centre of Jewish identity, a law which Christ did not reject, and the new law of grace given freely to all in Christ.

Justice is not the same as charity. Both are needed. Charity is optional: we can choose to give from our plenty to those who have less. Justice is about giving people something that is due to them because they are human beings, something that they need in order to be fully human: food, shelter, education, health care, social relationships, employment and so on.

Justice work focuses both on individuals and on the structures that block people from living life to the full.

Work for justice also challenges false ideologies, such as nationalism

– be it British or Irish, unregulated capitalism, state socialism that does not respect individuals, consumerism, patriarchy and other forms of gender discrimination, lack of respect for disabled people or people with special needs.

In speaking in the way he did Christ followed the language and actions of the Old Testament prophets. Everyone is not called to be a prophet. A church without prophets, however, is not the church of Jesus Christ. Prophecy exposes wrongdoing, challenges the wrongdoer and calls for costly change. This will always involve conflict.

Outcasts

Christ was a disturber of the peace. His actions were shocking. He would greatly disturb our modern churches.

A shocking act was to have table fellowship with the tax collectors. They collaborated with the Roman occupiers and polluted the holy places of the Jewish people. In doing so the tax collectors offended people not only politically but also spiritually. On top of all this they seized as much money from people as they could. The people, many of who were subsistence farmers, and none of who had state benefits, had to pay, or else face the wrath of the Roman occupiers.

Eating with people in Middle Eastern culture is not only about food: it is about relationship, respect and hospitality. It is difficult for us to imagine the impact of Jesus doing this with tax collectors. An analogy might be Brian at the height of Troubles (in Northern Ireland) taking part in an Ulster Defence Regiment (UDR)[2] hosted meal in the centre of Portadown, or Tim joining in an Irish Republican Army (IRA) commemoration. Either of these, for different reasons, would have been deeply offensive to many in our respective congregations. One thing about Jesus is certain: he did not come to please everyone.

A second group he was constantly accused of accepting was prostitutes. Prostitutes in most societies get named as sinners, and for good reason. They contribute to breaking up relationships. They sell sex. Yet, for the most part they are presented as if they had sex on their own: the men are invisible. That was precisely what Jesus exposed in his encounter with the woman in John 8: the Pharisees dragged her before him, pointed out that the law required her to be stoned, and then asked him to respond. Jesus at first said nothing, but knelt down and wrote on the ground with his finger. We do not know why he did this. Was it to be on the same level as the woman, if the men had flung her on the ground? And then he says, in that earth-shattering sentence which has echoed down the centuries wherever self-righteousness abounds, 'Let him who is without sin cast the first stone'.

Many of Jesus' actions and parables are aimed at exposing an underlying truth: in this case that prostitution between men and women only exists because men pay for it – and often impose it, as in the case of trafficked women. We are told that all the men left, one by one, starting with the oldest. Jesus is left alone with the woman. 'Has no one condemned you?' he asks, and when she replies 'no one', he says: 'neither do I condemn you . . . Go away, and from this moment sin no more' (*Jn.8:1–11*): compassion, respect, a call to live life to the full and a challenge to oppressors who were initially invisible because of patriarchy – all are there in this remarkable incident.

The shocking thing about Jesus' relationships with outcasts is that he did not wait for their repentance. On the contrary, as St Paul says, 'Christ died for us while we were still sinners' (*Rom.5:8*). The tax collectors with whom he ate had just come from their oppressive work, and most were going right back to it. Further, the meals were paid for out of the taxes that they levied. Yet, Jesus entered into table fellowship with them.

Jesus' public ministry was in the towns and villages of Galilee, all outside the centre of power and influence. He did not go to the centres of power. There is no mention of him visiting Sepphoris, the new Roman city built shortly before his birth only a few miles from Nazareth. This is surprising. The building of the city must surely have attracted workmen from all the surrounding districts, including Joseph.

Repentance

At the very start of his preaching of the Kingdom Jesus insisted on the need for repentance, 'the Kingdom of God is near at hand. Repent, and believe the gospel' (*Mk.1:15*). To repent is to admit our sins and to ask God to forgive us. But it does not stop there, as genuine repentance means changing and living our lives according to God's will. To repent is not simply to be sorry for our sins in any trite way, or even to lament their impact on others. It involves a change of heart and a change in behaviour: 'In truth I tell you, insofar as you did this to one of the least of these my brothers or sisters, you did it to me' (*Mt.25:40*).

We often think of repentance as something we have to do as individuals. However in the Bible the community is also confronted with the need of it. The chosen people constantly turned away from social justice and it was as a people that they had to seek forgiveness (*2 Chr.6:38*). Without admitting guilt and seeking forgiveness they could not return to the covenant community. The New Testament likewise almost always talks of the community rather than the individual – in all of Paul's letters, for instance, the word 'you' only once appears in the singular. Our concern, bordering often on obsession, with the individual, although not without its insights, is a post-Enlightenment phenomenon.

Communities and Churches, as well as individuals, are called to conversion and repentance, to confess the manifold failings which have contributed to our present mess. The call to repentance is as urgent today as it was for the chosen people and for those who first heard the Lord proclaim the Kingdom of God, but too often we apply it to others, not to ourselves. Failure to repent, both as individuals and as Churches, is a basic reason why our Churches lack so many of the marks of the Kingdom of God.

The cross and the failure of Christ's mission

The cross was the last thing on earth that Christ wanted. It was the ultimate failure of his mission. What he wanted instead was that people would repent, that they would put the love of God and of each other at the centre of their lives, that they would reform the law so that it would bring people freedom and not unnecessary burdens, that they would look after the widows and orphans, that they would rejoice and celebrate friendship and that they would confront wrongdoers but also offer them forgiveness. For the most part none of this happened. Instead he was rejected by his own people, betrayed by his closest friends, crucified by the Romans at the insistence of the leaders of the people and experienced being abandoned by his Father.

This was the exact opposite of success. Yet, from the very beginning, the followers of Christ rejoiced in the cross. It was through the cross that they, and the world, had been saved. How has the cross become the means of our salvation? Why was it necessary?

Christ, the God-human, by entering into our world and living a life of sacrifice not for his own sake but because of his love for his brothers and sisters, has entered into solidarity with all suffering human beings. He has shown us the possibilities of love. In doing this he has shown us our true reality: creatures called through our love for each other to share in the inner life of God.

In this sense he has overcome sin – that which separates us from each other and from God. He has broken down the divisions which limit the full flowering of our humanity (*Eph.2:14*).

On the first Good Friday the curtain of the temple, which separated the Holy of Holies from the mass of the people, was torn in two (*Mk.15:38*). The Kingdom of God broke, thus, into all aspects of life, and was no longer confined to the locale of the temple.

Conquering death

After the murder of Jesus his early followers were in a state of absolute despair and fear. Their dream, that Jesus would free them from the Romans, the tax collectors and the religious oppressors among their own people, was shattered. They describe in different ways a process that changed their lives forever. Through this process they experienced Christ not as dead but as alive. No one saw the resurrection. Different witnesses in different times and places gave testimony about encountering him. There were common themes to many of these: he was the same Lord that they knew before his death, but often they did not recognise him at first; he was physically present but appeared in rooms with locked doors; he disappeared as mysteriously as he appeared; their hearts were wild with joy; they changed from people filled with fear to utterly fearless preachers of the incredible news that Christ was alive. They spent the rest of their lives consumed with a desire to let others know this news. Many gave their lives in this effort, and both they and their companions saw this, not as a disaster, but as a joyful entering into the suffering of Christ so that they might share his glory.

The earliest witnesses to the risen Christ were the first to pass on the news. Yet, the figure who set up the structures of a Church that was to last down the centuries was St Paul, and he had never met Christ during his life. He did not show much interest in the human life of Christ. His main focus is on the risen Christ. It would be twenty years or more after Paul's letters before the gospel stories about the life of Christ would be written.

Belief in the resurrection was problematical for many Jewish people. Belief in any form of afterlife had probably only emerged, at least in part, through contact made with Persian religious traditions during the previous 300 years, and was a major source of disagreement between the Sadducees, who did not accept the idea, and the Pharisees, who did (*Mt.22:23-33*). Prior to the emergence of a belief in some form of resurrection there was little to look forward to in the next life, other than the shadowy half-life of '*Sheol*' (*Ps.6:5;116:3*).

The Christian community sided emphatically with the Pharisees in this debate: there was an intense feeling that the life that was in Jesus was stronger than death (*1 Cor.15*) and that those who had been baptised 'into Christ' shared in the new life of his resurrection (*Rom.6:1-10*).

Two problems are common when thinking about the resurrection. One problem is that the resurrection is so familiar to us that we lose the sense of awe. If Christ really is alive, then this is the most astonishing thing that has ever happened. Further it shows that he really is one with God, that God really exists and that God loves us beyond our wildest imaginings.

A second problem is that we are not sure about the resurrection. In the culture we live it is easy to be agnostic: maybe there is something in the story and maybe there isn't. That feeling blocks our awe as much as our over familiarity with the story can. It also undermines our joy in the risen Christ and our commitment to him.

To have awe and wonder in the resurrection, and to have the commitment to Christ that flows from these, does not mean we need to express our belief in an overtly evangelical way – although many will find that helpful. It does mean, however, that we need to find a way to express our joy both individually and communally. 'Joy' here is not a shallow emotion: it is more a deep and abiding sense that God in Christ is with us and that we belong to Christ. The purpose of expressing this is not simply for others: it is for ourselves. If we have this joy we need to find a way to express it. How we do that will differ for each one of us.

Both of us think this expression of individual and communal joy is important. It comes with an important theological weight. The issue of how we express joy needs to be addressed, partly in order to deal with the phenomenon of the bland God. One person we might turn to, to address it, is Anselm, who wrote in the eleventh century.

Building on the work of St Augustine, St Anselm expounded a view of the work of Christ which has become the default position of most of the Western Church. In his *Proslogion* and in his equally influential *Cur Deus Homo* (1098) he argued that we, through our sin, alienated ourselves from God. In order to restore that fractured relationship we needed, as human beings, to offer something adequate to God. Yet, as human beings, there was nothing adequate that we could offer. Only God was adequate to God, and only God was able to overcome the division created by sin. Therefore, only a person who was *both* God and human could offer something adequate to God. The argument seems almost too neat.

Anselm's thinking is typically nuanced and wise, unlike many of his interpreters in more recent times. His sensitive and inclusive theology, which argued for the necessity of the incarnation, has been crudely extended to suggest that the self-sacrifice of Christ was necessary to appease the righteous anger of an angry God. This idea, often referred to as 'substitutionary atonement' or, in its more extreme form, as 'penal substitution', has become the default theological position of many, particularly evangelicals, since the latter years of the nineteenth century.

The problem with this idea is fivefold:

◆ It suggests an angry and inflexible God at variance with the God revealed in and by Jesus Christ.

- It suggests a cold legalism at variance with any picture of God as three persons deeply in love with each other and with all human persons.
- It begs the question as to what sort of God would kill his own blameless son. Such a God is a million miles away from the New Testament God of love.
- It is too mechanical, forgetting that there are people involved on all sides.
- It uses a sacrificial model that has little resonance today for a society in which cultic sacrifice is, at most, an historical curiosity.

However, if we casually dismiss the Augustinian–Anselmian consensus of substitutionary atonement, we risk diluting the faith. The New Testament is full of references to Christ dying for our sins. Why did Christ have to do this, however? If God is merely an angry God, God is hardly attractive but if God is never angry, and does not need to be appeased, then where is God's justice? Further, what is the point of the incarnation and crucifixion? They are not needed, since we are made right with God, by God simply overlooking or forgetting about our sins. And what does this say to the people that we have hurt?

Channels along which a solution (a thoroughly Anglican middle way?) might be found are:

- The incarnation shows us the 'human face of God', the real possibility of a life well lived in harmony with both God and other people.
- The crucifixion was not a necessary appeasement of a demanding deity (a thought that would have come easily to those used to a sacrificial system such as was common both within Israel and among her neighbours), but God's way of expressing sorrow at the imperfections that had crept into his

wonderful creation. It was as though God was saying: 'Look, I am alongside you in this mess.' The powers of darkness have no hold.

◆ Jesus, the incarnate word and wisdom of God, was a representative person, existing for others in self-surrender. He is the one who steps aside from glory and stands up for others. He identifies with fallen humanity. His representation has a unique and universal significance, through which the world is reconciled with God.

◆ Jesus, the full human being, is the one person who lived human life to the full. By doing so he gave glory to God: 'glory' here means not a self-aggrandisement of the deity, but the passionate dance of a loving God filled with joy at human life lived to the full. In his full life Christ overcomes the separation between God and humans by bringing humans into harmony with God's love.

If these lines of thought are followed through, we find that God becomes both accessible and transcendent, loving and demanding. Jesus is the one who sets us an example that is comprehensible in human terms – an example that inspires (or should inspire) a similarly loving, forgiving and inclusive response; a response that needs to be seen in our personal lives and in our interpersonal relations (in other words, in the broadest sense, in our politics).

Chapter 3: How Did Our Lord Do All This?

By being immersed in the life of people

Our Lord moved around Palestine during his public ministry and stayed in people's houses, for example with Peter, with Mary and Martha of Bethany and with Zacchaeus the tax collector. He told them stories that they recognised from their own work and homes: the sower, the good shepherd, the lost coin, the rich man and the raising of Lazarus. There was no sign in this of a magnificent bishop, attached to his palace, or of a remote guru.

By spending long hours at meals with people

Jesus ate with Martha, Mary and presumably his friend Lazarus at Bethany; with Peter's mother in law after he had cured her and with the tax collectors (often, compare *Lk.11:37* and *Lk.14:1*), including Zacchaeus (*Lk.19:6*). He also ate with the two men on the road to Emmaus (*Lk.24:13-35*). Meals figure in many of the resurrection stories (*Lk.24:36-43* and *Jn.21:15*). There was also the miraculous feeding of the crowds in John 6, Matthew 14, Luke 9 and Mark 6. There is the story of the great banquet in heaven when many will come from the East and the West – outsiders, and the poor, the maimed, the blind and the lame will be brought in (*Lk.14:15-24*). Even those who do not seem to be eating at table with him can find pardon, community and forgiveness at the meals that Jesus attends, like the woman who wipes his feet with her hair (*Lk. 7:36-50*). Mary of Bethany anointed his feet at a meal shortly before his Passion (*Jn. 11:1-4*), and Jesus sees her action as one of great love springing from her realisation that her sins have been forgiven. He taught his disciples to pray to their Father for food, 'Give us today our daily bread' (*Lk. 11:3*), and to eat and drink what their hosts offered them, when he sent them on their missionary journey (*Lk. 10:7*).

The emphasis on meals is very strong, especially in Luke, so much so that some accused Jesus of being a glutton and a drunkard (*Mt. 11:19*). In part this is an aspect of Middle Eastern communal hospitality. The meal was a sign of friendship, a guarantee of safety. The stranger by accepting it undertook to respect the host (*Gen. 18*).

These meals were also echoes of the Old Testament Jewish world of sacrifice to which Jesus belonged. Covenants were confirmed by sacrifices, followed by meals, and at important points in the nation's history – for example, the renewal of the covenant at Mount Ebal (*Deut. 27:1-8*), the coronation of Saul (*1 Sam. 11:15*), the movement of the Ark to David's tent (*1 Chr. 16:1-3*), and the dedication of Solomon's temple (*2 Chr. 7:1-10*)[3].

St Paul tells us to have the mind of Christ (*Phil. 2:5*) not that of the world around us. Jesus never faced the choice between an iPhone and an Android. We do. We can have balance in our personal and communal lives, if we so choose. The image of a family, or friends, eating and sharing together is the very opposite of that of a group sitting together, texting to the world but absent from each other.

By healing the sick

The gospels are full of stories about Jesus healing people:

- ◆ The paralytic person in Luke 5 who is carried by his friends and brought to the house where Jesus is preaching. We are not even told that he wanted this. He did not ask for it (could he speak at all?). It was his friends who took the initiative. There was no room in the house, so they hauled him up on the flat roof and, having taken the tiles off the roof, sat him down in front of him – how terrifying an experience was this for the paralytic person? Jesus shocks his listeners by forgiving the paralytic person his sins. 'Who can forgive sins but God?' he says, showing here that the divinity of Christ is not simply a Pauline invention. Then he healed him. Only then did the paralytic speak, and he spoke to give thanks and praise to God.

♦ The woman healed of the issue of blood in Luke 8. She had lived with her problem for twelve years. Not only was it a medical problem, it also made her 'unclean' and this meant she could not take part in religious ceremonies. She was excluded from most significant communal events in her society. She touched the hem of his cloak and instantly she was cured.

♦ The man born blind in John 9. Jesus healed him, even though he had not asked to be healed.

Faith in one form or another is common to all the healing stories. Faith here means a hope in Christ, a turning towards him, and a building of a relationship with him. In the case of the paralytic person the faith shown in the story initially is not his own, but that of his friends who had brought him to Christ. The woman turned towards him out of desperation. The man born blind in John 9 had not asked for healing, but in the story, after his cure, he believed in Jesus when Jesus told him that he was the Son of Man.

Those who seek healing in our Churches often look for miracles. Yet, in the synoptic gospels the healing stories fade in number as the gospels proceed. There is no healing during the Passion. 'My God, my God, why have you forsaken me?' produces no apparent response from the Father in heaven. In the Gospel of John the miracles are significant only as signs – as pointers to the real identity of Christ. So, at the pool of Siloam in John 5 the man is healed, but he does not come to faith. This is in direct and deliberate contrast with the man born blind in chapter 9.

Our Churches, then, are right to pray for physical healing, but we also need to pray for the deeper healing that leads us to a relationship with Christ.

By teaching

Jesus is often called 'rabbi', or 'teacher' in the gospel because he spent so much time teaching. Much of his teaching underlines and to some extent reinterprets Old Testament teaching on the covenant community. Some of it is new, especially the move from 'an eye for an eye', to 'love your enemies' (*Mt.5:38-44*). He also taught with authority, unlike the scribes (*Mk.1:22*). The people were amazed at his teaching. Why? In the Old Testament prophets always referred to what Yahweh said to them, but Jesus said 'I say unto you…'. Certainly part of the reason for their amazement was Jesus' relationship with his Father. It was not only that he proclaimed this relationship, but what this relationship did to him as a person. While the scribes relied on the law, Jesus relied on this relationship. He also challenged the additions to the law that had crept in with time. He was seen, even in his lifetime, as a great prophet. The disciples told him people thought he was John the Baptist, or Elijah, or Jeremiah or one of the other great prophets come back to life. The gospels present him as the new Moses, the greatest of all the prophets.

With humour and compassion

Jesus had a sense of humour. Too many people overlook this, partly because they have an idea of holiness as something straight laced. It would be impossible for Jesus to enjoy so many meals with his friends, and even with tax collectors, unless he had a sense of humour. Do we think he sat solemnly through all these meals?

It is also hard to imagine Jesus and his disciples not enjoying a bit of light-hearted banter as they travelled around. Again and again Jesus' warm humanity is revealed: part of this warm humanity is humour. He would not have been fully human had he not enjoyed a good laugh, and the disciples would not have stayed with him had life with him been free of laughter.

Jesus' compassion stands out again and again. The miracles were signs, pointers, to his divinity. They were also, however, responses to people's suffering. When he went away to a quiet place with the disciples after the murder of John the Baptist the crowd guessed where he was going and got there before him. Yet, despite his need for respite we are told he had compassion on them 'because they were like sheep without a shepherd' (*Mk. 6:34*). He had compassion on the two blind men outside Jericho (*Mt. 20:34*), on the lepers (*Mk. 1:40*) and on the woman whose son was being buried in Nain (*Lk. 7:12*). In the story of the prodigal father (*Lk. 15*) he demonstrated his compassion, as he did in many other instances.

Indeed it can be argued that compassion was the single strongest character trait in Christ. His anger at the scribes and Pharisees sprang from the compassion he felt for their victims. He even had compassion for the tax collectors who were oppressing his people.

If we want to know what God is like we can look at Christ, who is the human face of God. He lives in his own person the loving kindness (*hesed*) of God that is such a strong theme for the Old Testament prophets. That compassion shows us the tender mercy of God. This is why Pope Francis has emphasised mercy so much, and why he calls for mercy in difficult pastoral situations such as that of people who have re-married, or who are gay or transgender, among many other examples.

By searching, questioning and being challenged

We have already mentioned that Jesus struggled with diversity and seems only gradually to have moved to a more inclusive vision of the Kingdom. But that move was possible because he was willing to dialogue with and be challenged by people, for example: changing his mind and deciding to cure the daughter of the Canaanite woman in Matthew 15; his astonishment at the faith of the Roman centurion (*Mt.8:14*); the apparent refusal to follow up on his mother's suggestion at the wedding at Cana, followed by his subsequent action (*Jn.2*).

We have also seen that Christ struggled with temptation. Temptation is something inside us. It disturbs us. We are pulled in conflicting directions. It destroys certainty. Christ, as a human being like us in all things but sin, had to search out his own calling and destiny. The miracle worker of the early gospels fades as confrontation grows with the Scribes and the Pharisees. The crowds thin out. He moves to the relative safety of Galilee.

With courage

Our Lord's courage is similar to that of many martyrs throughout history. Courage is not about the absence of fear. It is about confronting and overcoming fear. It seems clear in the gospels that Jesus avoided Jerusalem for much of his ministry because he feared being attacked there by the religious leaders. His early temptation was to be a magician, to turn the stone into bread. When he began to think about his suffering and death he told his disciples of his thoughts. Peter tried to reassure him, telling him that such a thing would never happen because Peter would protect him. Jesus' vehement response, 'Get behind me Satan' (*Mt.16:23*), shows how much of a struggle was going on within him. Had he not been conflicted about going to Jerusalem his response to Peter would have been mild and dispassionate. Why did Christ react so furiously? Peter had touched on the struggle within Christ, and in doing so had touched on Christ's doubts and on his vulnerability. Our Lord's overreaction shows that he was still struggling with his decision: whether to stay away from Jerusalem, the place of power and prestige, and also the place where the prophets were killed, or to face into confrontation and suffering. The scene also shows the depth of the relationship between our Lord and Peter: it is our friends who intuitively touch the raw buttons deep inside us, and we can lash out at our friends because we know they will not walk away – although it would only be after the resurrection that this could be truly said of Peter.

Then we see him broken in spirit at the Agony in the Garden of Gethsemane. An agony which ended not with a flight from his destiny but with its confrontation. His decision had been made earlier when he turned his face towards Jerusalem, a decision that Luke presents in stark terms (*Lk.9:51*), but that decision had to be reaffirmed in the garden.

We see the same struggle at the Agony in the Garden: 'Father, if you are willing, take this cup from me. Nevertheless, let your will be done, not mine' (*Lk.22:42*). He wanted to avoid the failure, the bleakness, the betrayal, the suffering and the abandonment of the cross. Yet, he also wanted to do his Father's will by living a full human life. He spent his whole life searching how to do this.

By forgiving sinners

The story of the prodigal father (*Lk.15:11-32*) is of a parent waiting day after day for the return of the son who has hurt him deeply. In the story, when the son reappears the father does not hear a word of the son's explanation. Instead he showers him with kisses and calls all his friends together to celebrate, 'because this, my son, was dead and is now alive' (*Lk15:32*). An important, and often overlooked part of the story, is that the younger son lets go of his own, quite accurate, image of himself as utterly unworthy to be his father's son. The last we hear (or see) of the younger son is of his standing on the road being embraced by the father.

After that, however, we can imagine his father bringing him into the house, laying out his best clothes, and preparing water in which he could wash. Then, with the neighbours assembled and all ready, the son walks into the meal on his father's arm, past all the neighbours standing to greet them, and up to the top table where he sits in the place of honour at his father's right hand. In so doing he accepts his father's view of himself. He lets go of his image of himself as a bum, and a waster. All that fades into the past in the embrace of his father.

That journey is possibly the longest in the world – letting go of his own image of himself and allowing his Father's image of him to enter into his deepest being. This is a life-long journey for all of us. It may also be what we will be doing for all eternity after this life is over.

There are other clues in the scriptures and tradition which go further than the story of the prodigal father who waits for the return of the son. On the cross Christ prays: 'Forgive them, Father, for they know not what they do' (*Lk. 23:34*). Is it likely that the prayer of Christ to his Father in heaven will go unanswered, and that God in the end will fail to bring all sinners into relationship with the three persons? If so, the whole plan of Christ, the longing of the Father and the love of the Holy Spirit will have failed.

In the creed we say: 'He descended into hell'. The theologian, Hans Urs von Balthasar, interprets this as meaning that God in Christ would not let go of those separated from God. Instead, the Father, in the Son, descends to their place of separation in order to stand alongside them, so that those who were separated from the Father would, through the Son, be brought back into unity with the Father.

This is a God who, while respecting human freedom, cannot let go of any single one of us. It is a God whose love, in the conflict between love and freedom, is ultimately more powerful than our human destructiveness.

There are many parts of the bible which point to God's desire to bring the whole world into relationship with God's own self: Israel is tasked with bringing God's salvation to the ends of the earth (*Isa.49:6*), in the book of Jonah the prophet's narrow nationalism is challenged by God's concern for the pagan people of Nineveh, the Book of Revelation pictures the new Jerusalem providing the light by which all nations will see (*Rev.21*) and the writer of 1 Timothy refers to God's will that all people be saved (*1 Tim.2:4*). Those who think of God as a punisher, filling hell up to the brim with sinners, grossly underestimate the desire of God that all will be saved, and the power of God's love to achieve this salvation.

Through prayer and worship

Again and again we see examples in the gospels of Christ turning to his Father in prayer: he prayed before the miraculous feeding of the 5000 (*Lk.9:16*), and again when he had sent the crowd away (*Mt.14*), he prayed before asking Peter who the people thought he was (*Lk.9:18*), at the Agony in the Garden (*Lk.22:39-46*) and on the cross. There are also several references to him rising early in the morning and going to a lonely place (*Mk.1:35*).

As a Jewish person Christ worshipped with his brothers and sisters in the synagogues and preached in them. He was nurtured in the Jewish tradition, undergoing its rites of passage (*Lk.2:21*) and celebrating its festivals even as a young boy (*Lk.2:41-50*). At times, we hear his Father responding, as at the baptism: 'This is my son, with whom I am well pleased' (*Mt.3:17*).

Through offering people salvation

The Scriptures are the story of God continually offering salvation to the people.

'Christ Jesus came into the world to save sinners' (*1 Tim.1:15*), and the Father 'wants everyone to be saved and reach full knowledge of the truth' (*1 Tim.2:4*). When the people grumbled because Jesus said he would stay at the house of Zacchaeus, a leading tax collector and therefore collaborator with the enemy, Jesus said that 'today salvation has come to this house, because this man (Zacchaeus) too is a son of Abraham' (*Lk.19:9*). It was precisely sinners like Zacchaeus that Jesus came to save, because 'it is not those who are healthy who need the doctor, but those who are sick. I came not to call the upright, but sinners' (*Mk.2:17*).

Salvation is about restoring the relationship between God and humans. In the Old Testament the people constantly turn away from Yahweh and his prophets, and the major theme of the journey from Egypt to the Promised Land is of Yahweh continuously forgiving them. Sometimes after strong persuasion from Moses, among others:

> '"So leave me now, so that my anger can blaze at them and I can put an end to them! I shall make a great nation of you instead." Moses tried to pacify Yahweh his God, and said, "why should your blaze at your people, whom you have brought out of Egypt by your great power and mighty hand? Why should the Egyptians say, 'He brought them out with evil intention, to slaughter them in the mountains and wipe them off the face of the earth'? Give up your burning wrath; relent over this disaster intended for your people' (*Ex.32:10-12*).

Salvation can be interpreted in many different ways. At its heart is the idea of healing ('*salve*'), which has traditionally been seen as a healing from the compulsion to sin and from the consequences of sinning. For most of Christian history sin has been seen in private terms, using the Ten Commandments as a personal and individualistic rule of life.

However, sin is far more than a personal inclination to do wrong: it is something that pervades society's institutions and structures at a deep level – the principalities and powers of this fallen world (*Eph. 6:12*). In order to be fully free as individuals and as a society we need salvation from structural sin as much as we need liberation from our personal peccadilloes. That is why faith and politics are so inseparably joined.

In the same way salvation is much more than forgiveness (important though that is). Central to any rounded concept of salvation must also be the ideas of freedom, liberation and peace. This last is a very poor translation of the Hebrew word '*shalom*', translated variously as wholeness, integrity, prosperity, favour, good health, rest, success and welfare: a rich concept indeed, giving us some inkling of what the Kingdom of God is all about. The Exodus gave the people of Israel freedom from slavery in Egypt. Christ Jesus, through his incarnation, passion and resurrection, offers to bring us out of slavery to all that oppresses us, and into the 'glorious freedom of the children of God' (*Rom. 8:21*).

It is thus clear that any biblically based concept of salvation must include the making of a socio-political context that frees us to live fully as a liberated people. We need to be freed in this way just as much as we need to be freed from our own personal sinfulness. In order for personal salvation to be experienced, we need to create a society that is freed from its own structural sinfulness. We need a society in which we have freedom:

- ◆ to express our own sense of identity
- ◆ to have adequately paid and rewarding work
- ◆ to have a home
- ◆ from injustice
- ◆ from unrealistic expectations

- from disproportionate rewards
- to celebrate what it is to be people loved by God.

Many of the things that oppress us today are financial and economic. Society is so dependent on the lubricant of money that most of us feel enslaved by it to one degree or another – having too much or too little, being in debt, just making ends meet. Money empowers: its lack dis-empowers.

This has always been the case, as it certainly was in Jesus' time. The preaching of the Kingdom of God included an economic dimension, for example, the petition in the Lord's Prayer that God forgive us our debts (trespasses) as we forgive those who are indebted to us. Debt and sin were, to Jesus, related concepts. The Kingdom of God (for which we pray in the immediately preceding petition) puts money in a new perspective – neither demonising it, not discarding it. At the heart of Jesus' living of the kingdom was his small group of twelve disciples, who needed money (and even had their own treasurer), but for whom money was hardly a priority. What made them work as a group (dysfunctional though they sometimes were) was the relationship they had with Jesus and with each other. This relationship was, in its own small way, a microcosm of the Kingdom.

At the heart of the Kingdom, at the heart of any meaningful concept of salvation, are relationships – relationships between individuals, between communities, between faith traditions and between religious folk and secular folk. Renewed relationships as modelled in the personhood of God – Father, Son and Holy Spirit separate but completely one in the harmony of love.

How can we be free, however, from economic and other oppressions when the money isn't there? A change in our attitude to money is one part of it. The importance we place on developing and improving our relationships is another. Having time for people is a third.

Working to change brutal financial structures that give a few people obscene wealth and crush millions is a fourth.

These are Kingdom values, the fruits of salvation, but they are hard to live out when we are exhausted by the pace of modern life, or ground down by poverty. We need to find a way not to let the oppressor get us down, of enthusiastically taking hold of this new world order and living it to the best of our ability; receiving the liberation of salvation with open arms and living it to the full. If we can have the courage to do this we can find peace – *shalom* – even in the most challenging of circumstances. Individuals can do this; so too can communities and whole societies.

By focusing on where we are ultimately going

Eschatology literally means the 'knowledge of the last things' – of the ultimate perfection that God wishes for God's creation. In the ministry of Jesus we see these 'last things' brought into present focus, and the values of the Kingdom of God brought into current reality (*Lk. 11:20*).

The gospels open with an urgent call to repentance, '"The time has come," he said. "The kingdom of God has come near. Repent and believe the good news!"' (*Mk. 1:15*). This Kingdom is not something only in the next life. It is a reality here and now. 'The Kingdom of God is within your midst' (*Lk. 17:21*).

So the Kingdom is, through Christ, already here. It is like a small grain of mustard seed (*Mt. 13:31*) in that it is insignificant to all but those of knowledgeable eye. Salvation through Christ brings that Kingdom down, realises that eschatological future today. There is here a tantalising tension between the already and the not-yet, a creative tension that can give life a new direction and meaning. It can also help us envision a better place here in Ireland and in the rest of the world. The Kingdom of God *is* among us. This truth is too often lost in today's world. In part this may be because it is expressed in alien terms. Eschatology is a long and forbidding word, and the concept of 'Kingdom' is also foreign to the political landscape of the twenty-first century. Gerhard Lohfink, in his powerful 2012 book on Jesus, prefers the term 'Reign of God', but even that is a limiting concept to today's mind. Either term is, at best, a shorthand for that place where and those people amongst whom the experiment of Jesus' values is being creatively explored; it is a shorthand for that counter-cultural but deeply liberating way of living that Christ Jesus himself demonstrated during his time here on earth. The 'Kingdom people' live out the values of the Kingdom in partnership and solidarity with Jesus Christ himself. The Kingdom is intensely personal, but also communal in its implications and impact.

Through being the 'human face of God'

It took time for the disciples to believe that Jesus was one with God. As we have seen, this was not surprising: for any Jewish person to see another human person on the same level as Yahweh was deeply scandalous. So at first they seemed to have seen Christ as a prophet – the gospels see him as a second Moses or Elijah, or else as the Messiah. This probably was not a divine title, but instead primarily referred to a new leader who would free them from oppression by the Romans. It also had implications for undoing social injustice. Yet, it also seems that quite soon after the death of Christ his followers were talking of him on a similar level to that of God. Paul, writing in Philippians about how Christians should live their daily lives, refers to Christ who,

'being in the form of God, did not count equality with God something to be grasped. But emptied himself, taking the form of a slave, becoming as human beings are; and being in every way like a human being, he was humbler yet, even to accepting death, death on a cross. And for this God raised him high, and gave him the name which is above all other names; so that all beings in the heavens, on earth and in the underworld should bend the knee at the name of Jesus and that every tongue should acknowledge Jesus Christ as Lord, to the glory of God the Father (*Phil. 2:5-11*).

And in Colossians, Paul says:

'He is the image of the unseen God, the first-born of all creation, for in him were created all things, in heaven and everything on earth, everything visible and everything invisible, thrones, ruling forces, sovereignties, powers – all things were created through him and for him. He exists before all things, and in him all things hold together, and he is the Head of the Body, that is, the Church. He is the Beginning, the first-born from the dead, so that he should be supreme in every way; because God wanted all fullness to be found in him and through him to reconcile all things to him, everything in heaven and everything on earth, by making peace through his death on the cross' (*Col. 1:15-20*).

Scholars believe each of these passages was taken from a pre-existent Christian hymn. Jesus also showed he was one with Yahweh by forgiving sins. 'Who can forgive sins but God alone?', the Pharisees ask when he tells the paralytic person that his sins are forgiven. Then, to show them that 'the Son of Man has authority on earth' he cures the paralytic person, who goes home praising God (*Lk. 5:17-25*).

While the Holy Spirit, in the gospels, is most fully dealt with in the Gospel of John, written about sixty years after the death of Christ, she is also present at the very beginning of the Christian story: Pentecost.

The doctrine of the Trinity emerged over several centuries because of the accounts early Christians gave of their experience. They knew Jesus when he was alive, they saw him crucified and then they experienced him as being alive once again – an experience that utterly transformed their lives. As mentioned, they used different terms to describe him: Messiah, Son of God, and so on Many of these were not divine attributes, but a ransacking of current superlatives in order to convey something of the impact that this man had on them. Gradually, however, they realised that none of these Christological titles were adequate unless they described Christ as being one with his Father. In the Gospel of John Christ is presented as one not only in deep intimacy with his Father, but as one with his Father. 'I and the Father are one' (*Jn.10:30*). For Jewish people – and the first followers of Christ were Jewish – to make such a statement was shocking. For Jewish people God is utterly transcendent, so much so that God's name must not be spoken directly. 'Yahweh' is roughly translated as 'I am who am'. Jewish people held God in utter awe:

Alleluia! Praise God in his holy place,

praise him in the heavenly vault of his power,

praise him for his mighty deeds,

praise him for all his greatness.

(*Ps.150:1-2*)

For these same people to conceive the thought that the man they had known, their friend and master, one with whom they had walked and whom they had seen butchered, was one with God was shocking in a way that we, their younger brothers and sisters, cannot imagine. Yet, their experience told them that Jesus was both fully human and one with God; that Jesus had sent the Holy Spirit among them, and that the Holy Spirit was also one with God; and that God was one.

The 300 years that it took for the Church to articulate the doctrine of the Trinity is a story of statements being made which slowly people realised were incorrect and which were then condemned as heresy. Each heresy opened the door to a development in the words used about God, so that eventually the Church arrived at statements about the Trinity and the Incarnation that were accepted as dogma in the fourth century.

We experience the Father as God, we experience Jesus as God, and we also experience the Holy Spirit as God. Yet God is one, and so what we experience is logically impossible. The perfect relationship of mutual love within the Godhead is no more than an attempt to explain both our experience and the mystery (or, as Rowan Williams would prefer, the 'difficulty') of God. That is something vital, in every sense of the word.

The teaching about the Trinity is at the heart of the Christian faith. God as three is a dynamic community of love into which we are invited to enter. We, as people made in the image of God (*Gen. 1:28*), only find our full humanity when we reconnect with God – a God who is more than an impersonal and indivisible unity – and when we relate to others in community as God relates both to God's own self and to humanity. God is not a hot line, a miracle worker, a divine Samaritan or a comforter to be approached whenever we feel the occasional need: God is rather the one who challenges us out of ourselves and into relationships that we might otherwise not have chosen. Relating to God brings answers, but it also brings a whole new set of relationships and questions. The Churches that we know reflect this all too rarely.

So the doctrine of the Trinity did not start as a dry theological thesis but rather as an experience of love that the disciples had with each of the three persons; an experience which led to the realisation that each of the three persons is one with God, and that at the same time God is one. At its heart, the 'doctrine of the Trinity' is not a doctrine at all, but an attempt to faithfully describe Christian experience.

The Trinity is a mellowing of the predominant image of God and not a dry and irrelevant academic exercise. It is the best insight we have yet come up with in over 2000 years to explain that which is, by definition, beyond our understanding – namely the nature of God. Experience of the multi-faceted nature of God came first, our clumsy attempts to define that experience came later.

God, as Anselm put it, is 'that than which nothing greater can be thought'. In other words, the concept of God is conceivable but the reality of God is not. Conceptualise God and we diminish and control God – that is why the early Jewish people made completely taboo the uttering of God's sacred name.

The 'doctrine of the Trinity' avoids this issue and points rather, as a preliminary and fallible explanation, to God as community. Even that is not enough: God is not an impersonal monad, beyond feeling, somewhere remote from his creation. God is a community of persons, warmly united in love.

It may be that we have lost a true sense of God's transcendence. We may also have lost a sense of the mystery that this transcendent God came among us as one like ourselves. To appreciate the utter wonder of the Incarnation we need to appreciate the Trinity. To appreciate the utter wonder of the Trinity we need to appreciate the Incarnation.

The idea of God as a trinity reveals, perhaps more closely than any other area of Christian thinking and experience, that we are in the realm of mystery. To invoke mystery is not to close the mind and resort to intellectual laziness, but rather to recognise the fundamental truth that faith is dealing with things that are beyond our capacity to understand. Faith, as Aquinas acknowledged, is qualitatively different from knowledge; it recognises that we do not actually know all that much *about* what we believe in. I do not need faith to believe that the table on which I am working actually exists, but I cannot prove that God exists with anything like the same degree of certainty. It is when we pretend to certainty, it is when we think that we know for sure, that we lose sight of mystery and risk falling into intolerance. We have to take the proverbial leap of faith and allow the communal, loving, inclusive and self-sacrificing God into our lives.

This picture of God – and it is only a picture – is important and has consequences both for the Church and for society. If we see God as warm, loving and relational we will organise ourselves very differently from the way we organise ourselves under the watchful eye of a policing God.

'The inner life of God' as a phrase can be spoken easily. Its meaning is not as easy to grasp. The climax of creation is that God created us in God's own image (*Gen. 1:28*). God's creation reached its fulfilment in Christ becoming human, in every respect the full image of God (*Col. 1:15-20*). This means in part that we will become like God (*1 Jn. 3:2*) but also that we will share in God's own life (*2 Cor. 4:10-11*). This is what being a brother or sister of Christ means: we are brought into relationship with the Son, and through the Son with the Father, by the power of the Holy Spirit.

There was, then, a pattern in Christ's life of friendship, teaching, healing, table companionship, personal prayer and worship. This, then, is the pattern for our Churches to imitate. How well do we do this?

SECTION 2: CRITIQUE OF CHURCHES

Chapter 4: Overview

Underlying ideas

The task of the Church is easily stated: to show the presence of God in Christ in the world. While we will always fail, this remains our calling: to work for the coming of Christ's community, and to do so with the values that Christ showed in his life.

In this section we want to critique our own Churches in the light of what we have highlighted as both the marks of Christ's community, and the way that he worked to bring this community about.

As we do so, there will inevitably be a change of tone. Our Lord's way of living and acting seems so attractive as we study it but when we come to apply that way to our own lives things become more difficult. We have to find out how Our Lord's life fits into our context, and in doing this we have to deal with our resistances. The more specific we make our critique the more likely we are to disagree. This is because the Church is catholic, or universal. If we all agreed on everything we would not be the Church. Many disagreements among us are valid. Yet, if we simply outline our Lord's life, and make no attempt to apply it to our own lives we remain at a level of vague generalisation: everyone will agree, but nothing will be real. Christ becomes significant when we dig into the nitty-gritty of life and ask what difference knowing him makes to us.

Covenant community, the Kingdom and idolatry

As we have seen, the Covenant was an agreement between God and her people. God would remain faithful to them, and the people would remain faithful to God. We remain faithful firstly, by worshipping her and by rejecting the temptations of idolatry and secondly, by loving our neighbour, in particular the marginalised. The Kingdom is Our Lord's own development of the covenant theme that was central to his Jewish faith. He saw the Kingdom as a new society based on respect, justice and forgiveness. It was not only for his own chosen Jewish people, but for the many who would come from the East and the West. It is a new society in which barriers between strangers are broken down. It is a society of outcasts, including the ultimate outcasts in that society: prostitutes and tax collectors. It is not just a spiritual kingdom, but one in which all our relationships are based on respect. The Kingdom of God is realised wherever these values are lived.

There are some obvious standards by which we can measure how well our Churches resemble the covenant community and the Kingdom. They are standards similar to those in Jesus' own day:

Who is included and who is excluded from our community? In Northern Irish language: who is one of ours, and who is not?

- ◆ How diverse are we in age, gender, wealth, denomination, sexual orientation, family, ethnic group, politics?
- ◆ How are the weakest in the community treated: children, elderly, the sick, refugees and migrants, foreign-born nationals, the depressed and addicts, those different from the majority in the parish?
- ◆ How much do we celebrate the gifts we have been given, especially the gift of knowing Christ?
- ◆ How consistent are we in applying kingdom values within and outside the Church?

Our Lord looks for answers not in words but in actions: with whom do we spend our time? About whom do we spend most time thinking? On whom do we spend our money and other resources?

First, a reality check: even in strong churches it is unlikely that more than fifteen per cent of the congregation will be active in church affairs. This is so because many are too busy rearing families, working long hours and studying, or are engaged in sport or other matters. Others want to take part in Eucharist, sacraments and church services but no more than that. Christ is incarnate – enfleshed – in a Church of sinners, so we have many gate keepers, power seekers, egotists, and status seekers to contend with too. All of us are sinners in one way or another. It is important therefore to accept that our Churches are never going to be perfect communities. We know only too well that even with the best will in the world not all that we recommend could be implemented. Nonetheless, both our Churches are in urgent need of reform and we need to find ways to engage as many in the Church as possible to bring reform about.

The Church has, particularly in recent decades, not been good at communicating the message of the Kingdom. Is there therefore a case for dispensing with our Churches and trying, simply, to live out our faith as individuals? That is a tempting but lazy option. It is tempting because our Churches have recently (and not-so-recently) been such spectacularly bad examples of kingdom communities. It is a lazy option, however, because such individualism flies in the face of what Christ preached. To slink back into the shell of individualism and pietism is to privatise a faith that can only thrive and have impact if it is lived communally, and in the public sphere. This need of a communal life of faith is reflected in the fact that the one God is a diverse community of persons.[4]

The world today needs a Church that engages radically with this Jesus and, at the same time, engages realistically with the world in which it finds itself. It needs to incarnate God incarnate. It is unrealistic to propose that the institutional Church be disbanded – every large and permanent gathering of people needs some sort of structure, and so suffers some form of institutionalisation. All institutions protect themselves. In this respect they can sometimes become complacent, too certain of their own worth and deeply unattractive to an impartial observer.

Any Church worthy of the name of Christ needs to follow him: as St Paul said 'Let this mind be among you that was also in Christ Jesus' (*Phil.2:5*). The Church must become a community of people, equal before the God who invites rather than coerces. It needs to become a community of people open to new ideas, willing to explore life and faith with all who are interested; a community not with all the answers (which have often been supplied before the questions were even heard) but, instead, with a willingness to explore the issues vital to people; a community living with the certainty of honest doubt, and which will not ask anyone to leave their minds and æsthetic sensibilities at the door of the church; a community which will allow the Christ we have experienced to mould our manner of being. To do this in an effective way would involve much prayer and discernment, under the guidance of the Holy Spirit, not least about our relationships with our inherited traditions.

Tradition
One of the great strengths of both our denominations is our sense of history, our links to our shared historic and apostolic faith, and our rootedness in the history of this country and the wider European Church. This gives a sense of security and timelessness, of being part of something deep in our personal, communal and national psyche. But roots can die and even the greatest truth can appear fossilised. What we have inherited is vital to our self-understanding and to the power of what we say but *our understanding of it* and *the way we express*

it can never be unchangeable. There will be times when cherished doctrines and ways of doing things will have to be rephrased – we will be attempting something of that later in this book. If our methods and our unwillingness to change are barriers to communicating the truth of Christ, then they have to change. We need, however, to get the balance right (something of an Anglican fixation!). Balance means respecting tradition, and struggling to find out what it meant at different times. It also means interrogating the tradition in the light of current knowledge and experience.

Churches in a changing world

This strange Church lives in a strange, varied and fast changing world. So, while the core of the gospel message is eternal, we need to tailor the way we communicate it to the society in which we find ourselves. So the way in which the gospel is formulated, the way in which Christ is preached, will be vastly different in Ireland than say, in Papua New Guinea where few local languages have any words for abstract concepts, and where the people find it difficult to grasp the concept of 'free gift', or grace. This was evidenced in the 1950s when Lutheran villagers in Papua New Guinea, who had been assiduous in their church attendance, and enthusiastic in their support of the Church, suddenly stopped coming to church. Enquiries were made, and the people explained that they were very grateful to Jesus for having saved them from their sins, but they reckoned that now, after so many years, they had given him adequate payback!

The Church needs to understand, or at least seek to understand, the nature of the various societies in which it finds itself. The better it does this, the better the Church will become at engaging with societies very different to our own, and to those with which the Church is readily familiar. Many of the theological disputes that racked the early Church during its first few centuries can be explained in part by the difficulties encountered as the gospel crossed linguistic and cultural barriers; translation, in every sense, is never easy.

Certainty and uncertainty

Are our Churches sellers of certainty or of searching? Certainty has its place in the life of Christians: we should know we are loved by God and that God will never let go of us. As so many of the Psalms say, God is our rock, someone on whom we can utterly depend even in our darkest moments. Yet, God is also mystery, and God does not lay out our path for us, either as individuals or Churches. We have to search for that, using the gifts God has given us of prayer, our brains and dialogue. We need to be a people sure of our certainty and certain of our uncertainty. Like Our Lord we need to learn from each other through conflict and confrontation. Accepting our uncertainty can help us with this. That is why we will never find the God of security that we often seek: God is far too mysterious to fit into our categories. Certainty is a dangerous thing. At its most rigid it can lead to a crusader or jihadi mentality, but even at a less extreme level it can lead to a casual dismissal of what is precious to others. It can be stultifying. Certainty, of the sort that thinks that it has arrived, that is has the right answers, precludes any kind of growth. We stop searching, we stop exploring, we arrive at a dead end. Certainty, of the sort so often espoused by all Churches, is something that says 'this is the only acceptable expression of truth', thereby excluding those who nuance things differently, or even disagree. That kind of certainty isolates the believer from those who believe differently. It makes it hard for us to ask creative and liberating questions. As Montaigne (1533–92) put it, in extreme form perhaps: 'only fools have made up their minds and are certain'. And that, sadly, is the impression so often given by Christians and their Churches.

Secularist challenges

Ours is a society that has, to a significant extent, lost its religious moorings. Many, especially those who do not go to Church-based schools, have little or no knowledge of the biblical stories that did so much to shape society's self-understanding in the past. Many children have no knowledge of the prayers their grandparents learnt in school. The past, to Tim's children's generation, is past. The Troubles in Northern Ireland belong to the same category as the First World War. The future is scary and uncontrollable. So let us eat and drink, for tomorrow we die. It is a society predicated on instant answers and the hope of instant gratification which can validly ask: 'if I live for the moment, why should Christ matter to me?' What can we say to our children that does not reek of complacent platitude?

Individualistic spirituality

Yet, our society has not completely lost a sense of transcendence; spirituality still flourishes among many. Much of what seems attractive to people in religion, however, is highly selective; they pick and choose the bits that they like and then fashion their own private 'spirituality', a separated 'self-fulfilment', difficult to distinguish from secular mindfulness. There are no roots, there is little knowledge of the Christian story in history, there is no context and there is little in the way of demand, or of belonging, except in the virtual world. It is a world of niche marketing. As a result, such smorgasbord faiths tend to last but a little while.

This is not to suggest that there is nothing positive in the spirituality of many young people. The spirituality of the past, with its deferentiality, authoritarianism and consequent abuse has spectacularly failed: young people have rightly rejected its oppressive aspects. There are also many examples of young people volunteering and working for justice. Much of this is done, however, without an awareness of the richness of Christian theology and spirituality. Our Churches have, to a significant extent, failed to communicate the vitality and integrity of Christ and the Christian tradition to this deeply unsatisfied world.

People are rational beings with a history and a context. So the message of Christ Jesus needs to be communicated in a way that makes it relevant to our minds, to our sense of identity and to the society in which we live, be that Ireland, the US, Papua New Guinea, or wherever. We can no longer rest content with framing our so-called answers in nineteenth century language, as though the world has not changed since the great evangelical revivals or the Roman Catholic ultramontane movement of that century and before. To insist on using outdated language and concepts is to insult both our hearers and our message.

Chapter 5: Our Experience of Our Churches

Our Churches have been the context in which we have discovered and grown in our own knowledge of Christ. Despite all that is wrong with today's Churches we would not be where we are without them. It is through the Church that both of us received our foundational, religious education: the faith has been passed on to us through the Church. We cannot become Christian, still less live as Christians, without some form of Church environment in which to relate to one another and grow. Churches have also been places in which we have experienced great kindness. It is striking how well clergy from quite different doctrinal backgrounds can work together, for example as prison chaplains, something Brian experiences regularly.

This has always been the case. The earliest Christians were just a group of people whose lives had been changed by Jesus. They did not think in terms of structures or organisation. But, as their numbers grew they were forced to organise themselves into a recognisable church, an *ekklesia* of people who had been 'called out' of society to preach and live the gospel of the Jesus whom they thought of as the Christ.

Gradually they began to think about the Church in theological terms – as the 'Body of Christ', the 'People of God', the 'Bride of Christ', a 'Light set on a hill' and so on. It was a spirit filled community charged to be ambassadors for Christ in an alien world. Over time, of course, this charismatic community became institutionalised, a part of the fabric of society and reflecting the failings of society as much as, if not more than, revealing the salvific power of Christ.

Yet, despite this, Christ is to be found in the Church, in its various manifestations, as well as outside it. The awful history of the Church is not a block to this, since it is in the messiness and sinfulness of the world that Christ chose to be incarnated and where he still reveals himself despite our most obstructive efforts.

The role of the Church in society

First and foremost the Church has a calling to be an evangelistic community, a witness to the values of the Kingdom of God. This can be manifest in many different ways, some of which are traditionally 'evangelistic', like missions, novenas, children's Bible Clubs and so on. For the most part, however, if local church communities think of themselves as evangelistic communities at all, it is in a low-key sense, seen in the form of open hospitality and in gentle hints that there is more to life than the merely material. The Church's *raison d'être* is to be the People of God: therefore it must, if it is to be true to its calling, reflect something of God in its daily life and witness. In their audit of their outreach work, churches need to ask if they are serving people in real need, and if they are doing this for purposes of conversion, or simply because the people they serve are human beings in need. Ironically, focusing on conversion is often guaranteed to put people off, whereas responding to their human condition, as Christ did so often, may open doors to faith.

Church is community

The Church is a community. It is more than a building. It can, and often does, offer a place of belonging in an increasingly fractured society. In the suburbs it is frequently one of the few organisations to which all generations can belong. In more rural communities it is a hugely valuable focus for social cohesion. When it works properly, this function is much more than just another club, for it is here, amongst these people, that folk are brought out of themselves and touched by God.

A place of worship

The church is a place of worship in which the sacraments are received, the Scriptures are read and expounded, rites of passage are celebrated, prayers are offered and a window into the things of God is opened. It is a place where, in the words of T S Eliot, 'we are here to kneel where prayer has been valid'. It is an oasis from the pressures of daily life. But, just as a physical oasis is where the camels stock up on food and water before continuing their journey into the desert, so too the oasis-like function of the church is not to be confused with a holiday camp or a luxury spa, cut off from the realities of daily life. The church is an oasis where we recharge our batteries, the better to live life to the full. It is a community in which the individual doubts and certainties of faith find their corporate expression and support. In the church we discover that we are not travelling alone.

A place for social and community activism

The church is also, and increasingly, a place for social and community activism. Sometimes this is parish based, with programmes for single parents, prisoners' families, the elderly, immigrants and the young. The Church is often used by governments to deliver services that the welfare state can no longer deliver. This is especially true in the USA where there is a strong tradition of volunteering, stronger than in Europe where the state plays a greater role in social relief. Sometimes, these functions are taken up by para-church organisations such as the Society of St Vincent de Paul or Food Banks.

In Ireland the Church plays a vital part in society. There is hardly a town or village without a number of churches strewn around its streets. The Church is involved in education and health care. It is heard on the media and is the occasion of frequently impassioned debate. Even today, in its chastened state, the Church is an unavoidable fact of Irish society.

Individualistic culture

We also work within a very individualist culture wherein what I want, and the way I interpret things are paramount. It is a 'me' culture in which the prevailing social norms are selfish ones. This is not to deny that there is much generosity and altruism around or that all of us gladly make small sacrifices for the greater good. But faith is regarded as a personal matter, and people do not take kindly to being told what to believe. So people tend to be very selective in what they choose to believe, and think it is not important if we all believe different things, an attitude strangely expressed by statements such as 'we all worship the same God'. That last statement is not a view that we share.

Individualism is fuelled by the advertising industry, which seeks to create a virtual community of individuals with ever-increasing desires. Why are shopping malls so full? What are people buying? How many socks can one go through in a year?

Christianity needs to find a proper expression in every culture, balancing meek acceptance of that culture with considered theological and rational criticism of its weaknesses.

We need to start the journey of faith as individuals, just as we talked about in the opening pages of this book. As the Scripture says, we need to 'love our neighbours as ourselves'. In other words, unless we have got our own personal relationship with God on some sort of even keel, anything we seek to do in the wider context runs the risk of being no more than a barren and empty shell. But there is much in all Church traditions that seems to be wrapped up in an excessively individualistic pietism and that needs to be challenged and broadened out.

Recent developments in society and in the Church have only exaggerated this. Religion is seen as a private thing; authority of any sort is frowned upon. Everything is relative, so absolute truth is hard to sell. People relate to each other less than they relate to their mobile phones and lap-tops: 'choose your own path because you are an individual, look to the modern world and forget about tradition'. Tradition, after all, has often disgraced itself.

Symbol of the divine, yet incarnated

It is the vocation of the Church to be the sign of Christ's community in the world. Clearly it does not always succeed. Yet, theologically, there are two sides to the Church: Christ's work and our human response. The first of these vastly outweighs the second. That is why it is important to state what the Church's vocation is: it is meant to be Christ's presence (or one aspect of his presence) in the world. The corruption of the Church shocks us and so it should. Yet, this again tells us something central about the God we worship: God has become flesh. God has come into our world not as it might be, or should be, but as it is, in all its brokenness and sinfulness. The statement that the Church is the sign of Christ's presence in the world sounds shocking only because we easily forget this incarnational reality.

We outlined in section one what for us are the most important elements in Christ's life. This outline is not simply based on our own experience: it fits the pattern in the gospels and in Christian tradition. The themes we outlined included: community – the community of the covenant, the Trinity and the Kingdom; the idolatry and sin that separate us from these communities; the inclusive nature of these communities – sinners and outcasts are welcome; the healing of the sick; the call to repent and the offering of forgiveness to all; the cross and failure of Christ's mission; the resurrection and vindication of Christ by the Father.

If we in our Churches are to fulfil our task of making visible the love of Christ in the Trinity, then we need to measure ourselves against these elements in Christ's life. How best can we fulfil our calling to be the sign of the presence of the Trinity in the world?

Chapter 6: Critique of the Roman Catholic Church
(Brian Lennon)

There is a tension at the centre of the Roman Catholic Church's understanding of Church structure. On the one hand the Church views itself through various theological ideas: the People of God, the Body of Christ and others. These are high ideals based on Scripture. On the other hand the Church is a visible organisation, made up of sinners, which has changed its structures of governance over the centuries.

Theological ideas, centralising power

Since shortly after the middle of the nineteenth century a renewed and determined effort was made to centralise power and authority in the Vatican, a process that arguably had been developing since the eleventh century. This saw its highpoint theologically in the claims of papal infallibility in the First Vatican Council. These were reaffirmed by the Second Vatican Council, but with a new balance emphasising collegiality. Effectively this meant that while there remained a recognition of the central role of the papacy there was also a stress on importance of the Church world-wide, as represented by the bishops, but also by lay people. The Council did this by changing the order of chapters in *Lumen Gentium*: the initial draft dealt first with bishops, then clergy, then laity. The final document instead started with the whole 'People of God'. Within that framework the different roles of bishop, clergy and laity were placed. That change was revolutionary: the clergy were no longer seen as the Church, but simply one part of it. The great failure, however, of the Council was its failure to set up structures that reflected this new balance. They left that to the Roman Curia which, with the strong support of John Paul II, and contrary to the spirit of the Second Vatican Council, reinforced centralism and clericalism.

Clericalism is caused primarily by ideas. Very early in the Church's history Christians began to think of Jesus as the new high priest. At the centre of Old Testament law was sacrifice: the people handed over to Yahweh one of the most important things they possessed as an agricultural people, their animals. The animals, and especially their blood, represented the people. Handing the animals over to Yahweh in sacrifice symbolised handing over the people.

Given this background, it was not therefore surprising that early in the life of the Church Christians began to see the cross in the light of Jewish sacrifice. The cross was Jesus handing himself over to the will of Father in a sacrifice on behalf of the people. Jesus was both the victim and the priest.

Legitimate and important though this interpretation is, there are problems with it. First, Jesus was not primarily a victim. 'Victim' has many meanings: all include the notion of a person being harmed. But harm can be caused accidentally or unintentionally, through an illness or by nature, as well as through deliberate injustice. A victim can also be understood as a living being sacrificed to a deity, or it can refer to someone who was duped.

Certainly Jesus was a victim inasmuch as he was murdered. That is not the same, however, as being a *sacrificial* victim. As we saw in section one, the last thing that Jesus wanted was the cross. The cross was the failure of his mission. So while the New Testament in places presents him as a sacrificial victim, it is not at all obvious that this is the way he saw himself. Passages such as Hebrews 9 and 10, although they use the language of cultic sacrifice, can be seen as Jesus transcending the Old Testament sacrificial system, once and for all. These things, the author is saying, are no longer necessary. Cultic sacrifice is no more.

Secondly, Christ was not a priest, at least not in Jewish terms. When the writer of Hebrews refers to him as the Great High Priest (*Heb. 4:14*) of the new and creative Order of Melchizedek (*Heb. 7:11-28*), or as the High Priest of the New Covenant (*Heb. 8:1-13*) he is following in the footsteps of many in the Old Testament who questioned the whole cultic sacrificial system: 'I desire mercy and not sacrifice' (*Hos. 6:6*; *Mic. 6:8*; *Am. 5:23*; *1 Sam. 15:22*; *Ps. 40:6*; *Ps. 51:16*). Melchizedek was not even an Israelite, but 'King of Salem and priest of God Most High', a priest for ever. This is a new kind of priesthood, not in the Aaronic mould. It is a priesthood that transcends anything that Israel knew.

To be a Jewish priest one had to be a member of the tribe of Levi (*Ex. 32*), which Jesus was not. Their task was to offer sacrifices in the Temple. Jesus challenged the corruption that grew up around the sacrificial system. That was one of the reasons why he attacked the money-changers in the Temple (*Mk. 11:12-17*). In doing this he was acting as a prophet. The gospels deliberately present him as working in the prophetic tradition of Moses and Elijah (*Mt. 17:11*). It is Moses the prophet and not his brother Aaron the priest who has precedence in the Old Testament story. The early Church in its struggle to make sense of the cross gave precedence to the image of Christ as priest over that of Christ as prophet. Then, in a second move, this precedence was subsequently applied to different officers within the Church. It was a short step from this to see clergy as superior to lay people and holier than them.

This does not mean that there is no argument for the development of the roles of deacons, priests and bishops in the early Church. These emerged fairly quickly. The evidence suggests, however, that giving precedence to deacons, priests and bishops *without reference to other members of the church* is not in keeping with that early development.

The balance that was present between the prophet Moses and the priest Aaron in the Old Testament has almost disappeared in the Roman Church. The image of Jesus as prophet receives almost no emphasis in the governance of the Church. As a consequence we have gradually developed a system where almost absolute power in canon law can theoretically be exercised by the Bishop of Rome over the whole Church, bishops over their dioceses, and parish priests over their parishes. Other baptised members of the Church, who are members of the Church just as much as the Bishop of Rome, have virtually no formal authority.

This is not the balance that St Paul called for:

> 'Now Christ's body is yourselves, each of you with a part to play in the whole. And those whom God has appointed in the Church are, first apostles, secondly prophets, thirdly teachers; after them miraculous powers, then gifts of healing, helpful acts, guidance, various kinds of tongues. Are all of them apostles? Or all prophets? Or all teachers? Or all miracle-workers? Do all have the gifts of healing? Do all of them speak in tongues and interpret them? Set your mind on the higher gifts' (*1 Cor. 12: 27-31*).

Priests are not mentioned in this list. Directing others comes seventh in the list. Prophets, meanwhile, are placed second.

Collegiality

There was much emphasis on collegiality in the first millennium of the Church's history, and thereafter in both the Orthodox Churches and the Anglican Communion. Developing greater collegiality was one of the reforms called for in the Second Vatican Council. Essentially it means changing the balance of power between the Bishop of Rome and bishops worldwide, and also between bishops, priests and laity. In a collegial approach the Bishop of Rome is seen as a member of the college of bishops, working with them, but also with a particular charism.

The Second Vatican Council was the first major experience of real collegiality in the church for nearly 100 years. At the start most bishops arrived with few ideas of the reforms they wanted. They quickly realised, however, that they did not want to accept the documents prepared by the Roman Curia in advance of the Council. They rejected them. That was the start of an extraordinary process in which the bishops discovered their own charism and voice. They moved from a vision of the Church centred on Rome to one centred on the 'People of God'. They also produced a series of documents each of which received overwhelming backing in the final votes. These documents, which contain many compromises, cannot therefore be dismissed or ignored by members of the Church.

The tragedy is, that having rediscovered the ancient balance of collegiality, the bishops at the Council failed to set up practical institutions to make it work. That was a mistake and the Church has suffered from it for the past fifty years. The Council spoke of the 'college' of bishops, but in practice this college has no independent structure, no mechanism to appoint officials, no secretariat, no process for meetings other than the periodical Synod of Bishops. Until the election of Francis these were controlled completely by the Bishop of Rome.

Pope Francis is certainly making great efforts to change this. Indeed, the Synod of Bishops on the family, held in 2014 and 2015, was one of the first real experiences of global collegiality since the Second Vatican Council. This was because the agenda of the Synod was not controlled by the Roman Curia. Francis had already introduced a new element of collegiality by asking the bishops to consult the members of their diocese about church teaching and practice on the family. While the nature of this consultation left much to be desired it was nonetheless a signal of the new focus on collegiality – including the laity – that the Bishop of Rome wanted to see.

If a workable college of bishops is to emerge it will need national or regional structures to underpin it: the most obvious candidates for these are the national conferences of bishops. John Paul II and Benedict XVI both opposed giving these any powers, but Francis has taken a different tack. On the contribution episcopal conferences might make to the correct relationship between primacy and collegiality, he wrote that the 'juridical status of episcopal conferences which would see them as subjects of specific attributions, including genuine doctrinal authority, has not yet been sufficiently elaborated. Excessive centralisation, rather than proving helpful, complicates the Church's life and her missionary outreach'.[5] The task of giving local bishops' conferences real power, and building from this to an effective international college of bishops is a considerable one. Given his age and health, Pope Francis may not have time on his side. Yet, without this change the Church will continue to be governed ineffectively from an over-centralised Rome.

For collegiality to reflect properly the charism of the People of God more is needed than an international college of bishops. Collegiality has to be effective at national, diocesan and parish levels. The Irish Bishops' Conference is not collegial. It lacks transparency and lay people have no effective legally recognised role. Rather than exercising its proper calling which is to act as a link between the People of God in Ireland and the universal church, it is seen as subservient to Rome.

The imbalance in the Church between priest and prophet is not only wrong, it is a key factor in many of the scandals from which the Church has suffered over the past twenty years. This is because central to clericalism is another deadly disease: *deferentialism*. Because of clericalism lay people, and other clerics, did not challenge those in authority who put the reputation of the Church before the protection of children. The clerical state, because it was seen, before the Second Vatican Council, in pre-Vatican 2 times as *higher* than any other, was seen to be more important than safeguarding children.

Much has changed in recent years. An *Irish Times* editorial in 2016 (6 May) expressed the view that in part because of the work of 'an army of lay volunteers and of the National Board for Safeguarding Children (a body which although funded by the Bishops' Conference has shown a large degree of independence), church-run organisations 'are now among the safest in Ireland for children'. The abuse scandals, together with rising secularism, especially in the Republic of Ireland, have dealt what is hopefully a death blow to deferentialism. Clericalism, however, remains strong in canon law, and in some other countries where child abuse has not yet been exposed.

Theological oversight

A second issue, related to over-centralisation, is the unjust way theological oversight was exercised. Rather than leaving this to local bishops' conferences it is the Congregation for the Doctrine and Faith (CDF) who takes on this role. The role is important: all Churches need a way to decide when members go beyond legitimate theological exploration. The means that the CDF employs to do this, however, can seem scandalous: the person investigated is often the last to know, the charges are often vague and general, the process lacks transparency and there is no proper appeal system. The Church cannot expect to be taken seriously in calling for justice in the rest of the world if its own systems are manifestly unjust.

Pope Benedict XVI, when still Cardinal Ratzinger, responded to this charge by arguing that it is statements of belief, not persons, that are examined by the CDF, so issues of justice in regard to human rights are not relevant. This is an example of idealist thinking: theologians do not produce their ideas from the sky. They come instead from many years of hard, personally committed work bound up with their faith in Christ. They are *personally* involved in their ideas. Of course this introduces bias. Yet, bias is present everywhere, including in the CDF. What matters is awareness of bias and acting to limit its influence. Besides, the trials currently conducted by the CDF, precisely because they show no awareness of the cultural and theological bias of investigators, and because they are secretive and non-accountable, are less likely to reach a measure of truth than a process governed by appropriately respectful laws. It is in part because disrespectful processes in secular law reached so many incorrect conclusions that governments, at least in the West, have introduced reforms to make law somewhat more transparent and accountable.

A people of God

As we have seen, the Second Vatican Council had a vision for the Church: that of the 'People of God'. Within that vision it saw different roles for lay people, deacons, priests, bishops, popes and others. All were part of the one people. This was a change from the previous view which had started with the Bishop of Rome and then addressed other bishops, priests, deacons, religious and lay people in that order. The Second Vatican Council's vision has not been fully realised. A telling example of this less than full realisation: some years ago, at the funeral of a bishop, the presiding bishop welcomed all the ecclesiastical dignitaries who were present, and then also welcomed 'my dear people of God', as if it was only the laity, and not also the clergy and bishops who were part of this 'dear people'. This issue goes back to what we have mentioned already: the focus on the priesthood of Christ to the exclusion of his role as prophet, and the transfer of this focus to the clergy. Consciousness of the Second Vatican Council's emphasis is changing within the Church, but far too slowly. Lay people need to claim and to be given leadership roles in the Church. Why, for example, should the heads of most Vatican departments not be lay people? Why is it assumed that ordination is a requirement to head, for example, the Congregation for the Doctrine of the Faith (CDF) or other Vatican departments?

Lay people wish to contribute to the development of doctrine. In fact this is happening, but not in a healthy way. Most Catholics seem to have rejected official church teaching in some important areas, such as birth control and living together before marriage. Considerable numbers, at least, have also done so on issues such as homosexual and lesbian relationships. One could argue that the Catholic Church in Ireland voted to legalise same-sex marriage in the civil referendum of 2015, because the proposal was passed by a two-thirds majority. Support for same-sex marriage came from rural as well as urban areas. Given that the level of Church practice in rural areas is higher, this suggests that a very considerable number of Church members supported the proposed change, against the opinion of their bishops.

As it happens, one of us, Brian Lennon, would have opposed the measure, not because he opposes gay marriage, but because he sees it as different from heterosexual marriage, a distinction that the wording of the referendum did not make.

It is incorrect to say that Church teaching never changes. It does, but often in a tortured way. An example is the teaching on wives obeying their husbands. From early in the church until the 1960s this teaching was proclaimed in many documents. The Second Vatican Council changed it by simply ignoring all the documents that went before it. That is often the way the Church operates: it fails to mention some teaching or document which it has used prominently in the past. But change it does. It would, however, be much healthier if there were structures in place through which lay people could bring their own experience to bear on the Church's response to new and often difficult questions.

Married clergy

The image of about 250 celibate bishops gathering in Rome for a Synod on the Family in 2014 and 2015 with only a few married people present, and in a consultiative role, was rightly criticised. It is wrong to think that celibates know *nothing* about families – we all came from one – but it is bizarre to suggest that only celibates should make decisions about marriage and sexuality in the Church. That is one reason why the Church should have married clergy.

Of course it already has: married priests in Eastern-rite Churches have been in union with Rome for hundreds of years, and others have joined the Roman Church as part of the Anglican Ordinariate set up by Benedict XVI. The life and work of these clergy, and of those in our sister denominations such as Tim's Church of Ireland, simply make the ban on other married clergy seem more peculiar. While scripture recognises the call to celibacy it certainly does not ban married clergy, unless St Peter and others are to be seen as non-ordained.

Bishop Krautler of Xingu diocese in Brazil raised the shortage of priests with Pope Francis in April 2014. There were twenty-seven priests in his diocese serving 700,000 Catholics. Francis responded that local bishops needed to be courageous in finding consensus in their bishops' conferences and in putting forward suggestions. The Pope could not handle everything from Rome. Shortly after this three British bishops said they would raise the issue at the next meeting of the hierarchy. In another signal, Cardinal Parolin, the Pope's Secretary of State, emphasised that clerical celibacy is a matter of discipline, not doctrine.

In March 2016 Pope Francis himself said he was open to the possibility of ordaining married people to address the shortage of priests in some countries.

In the US, married men have acted as deacons for many years. This has happened only recently in Ireland. There might be a hope that as people get used to the idea of married clergy – deacons are clergy – further questions will be raised as to why married people cannot be ordained priests. Yet, despite having had married deacons for many years in the US, few bishops there have called for married priests.

The shortage of priests makes the issue increasingly urgent. Clustering of parishes – the current response to shortages – may work for about ten years. After that parishes will be denied the Eucharist unless new candidates are ordained. It is encouraging that at least one Irish bishop, Leo O'Reilly of Kilmore, called in June 2015 for the issue of married clergy to be on the agenda of the bishops' conference. Why is it that the Irish Bishops' Conference, and bishops' conferences around the world, are not more urgent in their engagement with this issue? Surely one of their main duties is to ensure that people can take part in the Eucharist?

Arguments for married clergy are not arguments against celibacy. Celibacy is a difficult calling, but so too is marriage. Both are calls to love, and without love humans do not grow and do not therefore reflect an image of our maker. Nor is celibacy a call to live without human relationships. Brian's faith in God, to a considerable extent, rests on his experience of his relationships, both with family and others. Celibacy is also a calling to a type of prayer different from that of married people. The Ignatian practice of early morning prayer is more difficult with kids waking you up early in the morning, or keeping you up most of the night as they teethe. Both experiences have their riches, and their difficulties. Celibacy is not opposed to marriage. Instead it is complementary. The Church, like the wider society, needs both celibates and married people, single and married clergy.

Women's ordination

The ban on women being ordained will be more difficult to change, but change it can. In this area Anglican and Protestant churches have the lead. They have shown how difficult change can be, but they have done it. For those in the Roman Church who oppose the ordination of women a significant question arises: if women cannot be ordained, and if all formal authority in the Church is tied to ordination, then women are excluded not only from ordination but also from significant leadership roles in the Church. How does this fit in with the obvious leadership roles played by people like Mary Magdalene – presented by John in his Gospel as the first of the apostles – and other women in the New Testament? Secondly, absolute conclusions need to be supported by very strong, and normally impossible, arguments. The thesis that God in Christ is opposed to the ordination of women in all places and circumstances is one such absolute argument. One might argue that in a particular time or culture women should not be ordained. That, however, is not the argument put forward. The fact that Jesus did not number women among the twelve apostles is often cited. The New Testament evidence does not make it absolutely clear that the subsequent leaders of Churches were seen as succeeding the twelve. The role of the twelve may have been primarily symbolic: representing the twelve tribes of Israel, and therefore the whole people of the world, in the Jewish view of the time.

Thirdly, where is the evidence to show that the gender of the Twelve was so central to Jesus' plan that he intended to exclude women permanently from priesthood? The crucial role that John and the other evangelists give to Mary Magdalene is also telling: she is named in all four gospels as the first to whom Jesus appeared, as the first to believe that he had overcome death, and as the first to bring this good news to others. For John, discipleship is *the* key role in the Church, and the most prominent person in this role is a woman. That is why in the Eastern tradition, and also in the teaching of John Paul II, Magdalene is seen as the apostle of the apostles.

That is why the decision by Pope Francis in June 2016 to upgrade Magdalene's memorial to a feast is very welcome. These things matter in the Roman Catholic Church. We have feasts for our major saints because we are putting them forward as models *par excellence* for Church members. It is striking that there are at least seven major universal feasts for Mary, the mother of Jesus, and at least thirty of lesser status, compared with the one memorial and no feast day for Mary Magdalen before the change made my Pope Francis.

One might argue that discipleship and priesthood are distinct, but in fact *all* the roles in the early Church emerged slowly, and often in response to new situations faced by the Church. The office of deacons was created because of the emerging conflict between Jewish people and Gentiles within the Church over the distribution of food. Whatever one's views on the ordination of women, it seems impossible to find in the New Testament the absolute evidence needed to support the argument that it should be banned for all time and in all circumstances.

In Ireland there have been calls for women deacons. In August 2014 Bishop Kieran O'Reilly of Killaloe in a pastoral letter invited men to apply for positions as deacons in the diocese. There was an outcry from many who had been involved in pastoral planning and work, especially women. They expressed surprise and hurt at the bishop's pastoral letter inviting men only to participate in the permanent diaconate 'to undertake work mainly done at present by women.'[6] Bishop O'Reilly listened, and in response postponed the invitation to men to apply for the diaconate. Subsequently, his confrère and namesake, Leo O'Reilly of Kilmore asked the Irish Bishops to set up a working group to examine the merits of ordaining women as deacons.

It is worth noting that while Paul is presented as refusing women any authority over men in the Church (*1 Tim.2:12*), one can and should ask if this injunction applies to all time, or if it is an injunction bound by the biases of the patriarchal society in which the epistle was written. Raymond Brown, a mainline Catholic scripture scholar, interprets 1 Timothy 3:11 as 'envisioning' women deacons,[7] and Romans 16:1 refers to Phoebe as a deacon. Further, in Galatians 3:28 Paul refutes any distinctions between men and women. Most scholars think the letters to Timothy were not written by Paul, but by a Christian community writing some time later. None of the scriptural arguments can be conclusive because of the difficulties of translating words such as *diakonos* in different contexts. This is precisely the point we have made above about absolutes: one cannot rely on scripture for absolute arguments about the ordination of women.

Education

Clericalism thrived when lay people were uneducated, especially in theology. This has been changing for many years. In the Roman Catholic diocese of Armagh approximately 100 people were engaged in some form of theological education in 2015, ranging from uncertified to degree courses. The learning of these adults will make an impact on the diocese. Some of these students have been ordained as deacons. Others play leading roles in diocesan commissions. The same is happening in some other dioceses. But, as always, more needs to be done. In particular there is a need for courses in working class areas because some people fear, incorrectly, that they have less capacity for education than middle-class people.

How will change come about?

The Catholic Church in Ireland will not change positively unless a significant number of its members work together and intelligently to bring such change about. A huge number of people are working for such change, and more calls for reform, which focus on the shortcomings that still exist, can be discouraging. Yet, we need to remember that the Church is, and always will be, in need of reform.

Irish bishops are called to be leaders of the Church. No one would envy them their task, but no one else can do the specific task to which they are called. In the nineteenth century Irish bishops were by no means deferential to Rome (one thinks of Archbishop McHale of Tuam), but since that time the opposite has often been the case.

A different picture can be seen in occasional reports of confrontations between the Irish bishops and sections of the Roman Curia. It is a great pity that these confrontations were not made public more often: they would have shown the bishops acting as part of the Irish Church and bringing the insights and challenges of that Church to Rome.

An example was the way the Irish hierarchy – and all the English speaking bishops – accepted the imposition of the new liturgy. (Tim's Anglican ears were visibly shocked when Brian read him some of the new prayers of the 2012 liturgy imposed by Rome).

An effective conference of bishops, with transparent and respectful processes in place, would help immensely. At times Irish bishops have set up impressive committees of talented and busy people, and then ignored their recommendations. Not only were some recommendations ignored; the process governing the response to them was shrouded in mystery and secrecy. It is time for the Irish hierarchy to develop more transparent and respectful procedures in this and many other areas.

To do that they need new structures, and these structures have to include significant lay input. The leadership of the Irish Church needs to be a leadership of the Church, not of a small minority. The task of the bishops is not to communicate messages from Rome to the laity. It is to be part of the bridge by which the Irish Church influences the worldwide Church, and the worldwide Church influences the Irish Church. The bishops are key players in this dynamic. They need, however, to become players who facilitate exchange, not bosses who impose answers to questions that have not been asked. Ironically, it may be that the crisis in the Church is so bad that leaders will be forced to change, and that is a sign of hope. That hope is strengthened by the leadership shown by Pope Francis in encouraging collegiality and dialogue, in his teaching on compassion, and in his communicating in such apparently simple terms to so many people worldwide. Far from simple, his communication is an extraordinary skill and gift.

Some argue that structural change is shallow; that what is really needed is more prayer and a deeper relationship with Christ. Of course these are needed. Yet, this argument is generally put forward by those who want to maintain a papal centralism, itself a structure that has developed progressively since the mid-nineteenth century. If structures really do not matter, then why is it important for them to do this? Secondly, as we have seen, the current structures exclude the vast majority of baptised Church members from participating in governance, and these structures were an important contributory factor to the cover up of abuse. Bad structures have done dreadful harm to the Church in Ireland. They are a scandal because they block the central task of the Church: to be an image of the presence of Christ in the world and be his partners in his mission.

An assembly of the Irish Church

As a preliminary step towards new structures that reflect the wider People of God, the Irish Church as a whole might consider the option of holding an assembly of the Church in the country as a whole. In this way the many voices that have begun to be heard can be brought together. Of course there are great dangers with assemblies. They can raise expectations and crush them because of the lack of follow-through. They have a mixed history in other countries. It is difficult to see, however, another way to symbolise the central change needed in the church: that it becomes a church of the People of God, and not of the clergy. Such an assembly should only be one item in a wide-ranging series of structural changes. The bishops, through an effective bishops' conference, could lead, facilitate and encourage this change but it will need concerted encouragement from organised lay groups in many dioceses to bring an assembly to pass.

An important item on the agenda should be to call for a change in canon law worldwide. An obvious target is Canon 129 which excludes lay people from effective governance in the Church. The assembly could also request the bishops' conference to act as if canon law had been changed and to devolve specific powers to lay people in diocesan and parish councils and other bodies. The conference cannot impose such decisions on individual dioceses, because under current canon law it has no power to do this. Decisions made at the level of the conference, however, will surely bring great pressure to bear on individual bishops to accept them. This will go some way to change the current situation whereby changes made by bishops or parish priests empowering lay people can be undone by their successors.

Secondly, given the terrible history of abuse in the Church in Ireland the assembly needs to satisfy itself that the Irish Church is following the highest standards. Lay people can play a critical role in ensuring that this question is answered by independent and competent judges.

Given also the positive changes that have been made in the area of abuse, the assembly should lobby within the Church for best practice internationally. This is crucial because it is about protecting children *today*. Where clericalism and deference thrive, children are more likely to be abused because clericalism and deferentialism put the protection of the Church first and encourage secrecy. Pushing for best practice internationally is also a way of preventing the myopia that gripped Ireland: many heard of abuse in Canada and the US but did not believe that it could happen here. We were wrong, terribly wrong.

Thirdly the assembly could petition Rome for permission for the Irish Church to have married clergy.

Fourthly, the assembly could, like the German hierarchy, reject the new translation of the liturgy and suggest ways to develop an alternative. One already exists: that of the 1998 International Commission on the Liturgy. Arguably there was far more diverse involvement of the international People of God in its production than in the current abysmal version.

Fifthly, the assembly might take seriously the teaching of the Second Vatican Council on Eucharistic hospitality. The *Decree on Ecumenism* in one sentence sees such hospitality as inappropriate because the Eucharist is a sign of unity and where unity does not exist sharing should not be encouraged. But *in the very next sentence* the Council says that the Eucharist is also a means towards unity and that sharing is therefore *sometimes to be commended* (Para 8). While Irish bishops have been strong in implementing the first part of this teaching, they have been woeful at the second. It remains a scandal that Tim, a priest of the Anglican Communion, cannot normally be invited to communion in the Roman Church.

Many are discouraged at the slow pace of change. Yet, change is happening. The appointment of Marie Collins, abuse survivor and long-term campaigner, to the Vatican commission on child protection in March 2014 would have been inconceivable had it not been for the long, hard campaign which she and so many others fought. Yet, she found the pace of change so slow that she chose to resign early in 2017. Her appointment and her resignation together point both to the progress that has been made, and the huge amount of work that remains to be done.

We saw above that lobbying in the Killaloe diocese led to the bishop postponing his invitation to men to apply as deacons. Cardinal Brady in 2013 accepted the election of lay co-chairs to parish area resource teams in Armagh, although canon lawyers might have argued against this. These examples are straws in the wind: the Catholic Church is changing in Ireland. Yet, these positive moves could be reversed by future bishops unless canon law is changed.

One reason why an assembly is important is that it could make recommendations on behalf of the whole Church in Ireland, assuming that it would be truly representative. More important than this, however, will be the process that precedes it and the structures it sets up to implement these decisions. Examples of collaborative dialogue within the Church have already emerged, among others in the dioceses of Armagh, Down and Connor and Killaloe. An assembly can build on these.

The above are only some of the changes needed in the Irish Catholic Church. They may not be the most important. Only the Church can decide that. Yet, a process is needed to make that decision, and the process can only take place if there are changes in structures and values. Whatever these changes are they will not return the Church to what it was in the 1950s. That is a good thing. Our age is different and the Church needs to develop for each new age, while still retaining its central essence.

The changes will not necessarily lead to huge numbers participating fully in the Church. The reasons for the fall in attendance are complex, and have much to do with secularisation. The reason why the Church needs to change is because it needs to become once more the Church – the People of God, the gathering of the people baptised into Christ's death and resurrection, who are called to witness to his love for the world by the way they act internally and externally.

Response (Tim Kinahan)

The Roman Catholic Church is changing fast, not least under the leadership of the current Pope, Francis. His style, as much as his substance, seems to be addressing many of the concerns that Brian has referred to above.

That statement actually sums up much of my concerns about the Roman Catholic Church: its over-reliance on the Pope. This is not just a question of over-centralisation (although that is certainly an issue). I find myself alarmed by the reception that the Pope receives when he goes to different countries, a reception which seems to go beyond mere celebrity status. There is an adulation there which seems unhealthy: for some in those crowds it is the person of the Pope who is important, not his message or the one he represents.

Of course, that is a danger that the Pope is well-aware of, but there is little that he can do to stop it. The reasons for this lie only in part in our celebrity and media-driven age. A deeper reason lies in the historic claims that the papacy has made for itself culminating in the declaration of papal infallibility: those claims are not easily side-stepped by viewing them as historical aberrations. Their cumulative effect is to place the papacy on a very unhealthy pedestal.

It is also worrying that one person can affect such radical change as is being witnessed today under Pope Francis. Things need to be more collegiate. There is real hope that Francis is moving in that direction, but there is no guarantee that his legacy will be respected if the next Pope has different ideas. Just look at the way that much of the legacy of the Second Vatican Council was put on the back burner. Brian's argument, above, that canon law needs to be changed to ensure this, is a powerful one.

I share Brian's concern about making celibacy mandatory for clergy. In October 1988 I wrote an article for *Intercom* (which describes itself as a 'pastoral and liturgical resource magazine' for clergy and religious published under the auspices of the Irish Catholic Bishops' Commission on Communication). It is, perhaps, worth quoting in full:

It is now nine years since my ordination to the priesthood in Saint Anne's Cathedral, Belfast. That is a special building to me, not just because of family connections, but also because I was baptised and made a deacon there.

During those years, and before, I have often wondered, half-afraid, whether I was called to celibacy. Of course, as an Anglican, there was no question of taking vows to that effect – unless I joined the Society of Saint Francis or the Community of the Resurrection. I am now rather glad that the denomination to which I belong demanded no such vow. Otherwise I would never have been able, on my return from a visit to the USA in July, to have proposed to the girl who is now my fiancée. Like every lover, I cannot stop talking about her.

I can see arguments for celibacy, at least on an intellectual level. To be married to the Church of God, to be the Bride of Christ, to be free from family responsibilities so as to fully dedicate oneself to the people of God – all these make sense. But I have never been able to make them (or any other such factors) into reasons for legislating on the matter. They have never been reasons strong enough to allow me to commit myself to the celibate life. And thanks be to God!

As we Anglicans see it, it is only the few – even among the clergy – who are called to this state. To say to a man (or a woman) that a whole range of options within the realm of human relationships are now closed to you is, as I see it, to limit their potential as humans, to contradict any valid theology of marriage, and to deny the givenness and beauty of human sexuality. Some may be called to celibacy, and may be made by God to find their fulfilment within it. But that must be something to which they commit themselves personally, and which they must be free to change without feeling that they have betrayed either themselves, or the Church, or God.

Of course, this is a very 'Protestant' position that perhaps over-emphasises the importance of individual freedom. It is also a 'Protestant' position in that it has grown out of my own experience, and has not just been accepted as part of the discipline of living as a servant of the Church. We mainstream Protestants, even us Anglicans, tend to be more flexible in our attitudes to authority than many (particularly Irish) Roman Catholics.

However, I would not accept that my attitude to celibacy is merely one of convenience. If doctrine can acceptably develop, so can attitudes and personal lifestyle. And the experience of our Church, and even of the Uniates within the Roman Catholic fold, confirm (at least as far as I am concerned) that for celibacy to be an *optional good* rather than a strict legal requirement is far better.

My personal attitudes have changed. Initially as a young priest I was attracted by the theory of celibacy, yet at the same time afraid lest God call me into it. Since I met Jackie, however, I have come to know in a way far deeper than I could ever have imagined, how incomplete I was as a person without her. I am not one of those who subscribe to the myth of romantic love, whereby marriages are made in heaven and it is only up to us to find and fulfil the heavenly intention; but I am now more certain than ever I was before that man and woman complement each other. There are undoubtedly some who can find completion in the celibate state, but I am not one of them. I thank God that I never had to commit myself to it.

It does worry me that the Roman Catholic Church requires young men to take such a vow at such an early age. In my own relationship with Jackie I have come to a wonderful and experiential knowledge of God that has confirmed, revolutionised and underpinned all that theology and experience has told me up to now. We have found within our mutuality a taste of what it is to be 'in Christ', and through him to be called to share something of the perfect mutuality that is within the Trinity.

If you would like some theological justification for what I have been saying, I believe it to be found, in root at least, in the early chapters of the book of Genesis. There man and woman, male and female, are both made in the 'image of God' (*Gen.1:27*); they are intended for union, to become 'one flesh' (*Gen.2:24*). In the union of man and woman, therefore, we receive a sacrament of that perfect unity in whose image we were all created. Jackie and I have been privileged, through our courtship and engagement, to glimpse something of this. Those of you who are married will no doubt know what I mean but in a way that we, as yet, are only just beginning to grasp.

Human love is certainly not the only avenue to such an experience of grace, and to such an understanding of the innermost identity of God, but it is a vital one. My faith, my life-experiences, and my theological training have all opened me to know human love from this perspective. It is an enormously enriching perspective.

Of course, and I cannot underline this enough, equally deep experiences of God come from him along many different paths. Before I experienced this, I also knew God in a way that was just wonderful. But now that knowledge is more wonderful still, coming as it does through every fibre of my being – through our embraces, through our kisses, through our sexuality and through the mutuality and give-and-take of being 'in love'. God has come to us *biologically*. Celibacy would have denied us that.

I also have concerns about the process of canonisation, which seems to use the wrong criteria. I have no problem with the idea of canonisation as such – it puts an official imprimatur on things and discourages unwise and short-lived local cults. But surely a saint is someone whose whole life has been dedicated to God, and whose life has radiated the love of God. To use miracles as a primary criterion for sanctification may trivialise the procedure.

There are, of course, doctrinal differences, but they worry me less, even where I have trouble with a specific doctrine (such as the Assumption of the Blessed Virgin Mary). I have become aware that God can and does come to people along paths that I find decidedly odd. This lesson was powerfully brought home to me during my three-year stint in Papua New Guinea. In addition to the many lessons I learnt there about cross-cultural communication, I also had to live an ecumenism within my own denomination. The Anglican Province of Papua New Guinea is one of the more High Church, or Catholic, provinces of the Anglican Communion, with practices and theologies that would not be seen in the Church of Ireland. Among these were the Angelus, priests being called 'Father' (and their wives 'Mother'), incense, sacramental confession and the reservation of the Eucharistic elements.

After the initial euphoria of the new, and when the isolation of the expatriate missionary life began to hit home, some of these practices began to grate on me. On examination I realised that, in most cases, the only reason they grated was because I was, after all, a bigoted Northern Ireland Prod at heart! Yet, one practice still makes me uneasy, and that is the reservation of the Eucharistic elements, because it seems unacceptable and over-literalistic to limit the divine presence. However, that still left me with the realisation that, even though I found this theologically unacceptable, others still found it a path to God and, more importantly, God could use what I found theologically unacceptable as a path along which God could come to people, people whose spirituality and love of God I respected. God is bigger than my limited understanding, or the beliefs of any one denomination. God can, and does, use what I consider mistaken to be an avenue of grace. Indeed, whenever I enter into a church where the Eucharistic elements are reserved, my theological reservations are swept away and I find it entirely natural and heartfelt to genuflect. Even in a Roman Catholic Church!

Chapter 7: Critique of the Church of Ireland
(Tim Kinahan)

There is much in what Brian has said about the Catholic Church that is also applicable to the Church of Ireland. While the Church of Ireland is not as centralised, either in theory or in practice, there is a real tendency (in some dioceses more than others) to embrace an over-centralised, over-corporatised administrative model.

Bishops

Part of the problem here is what we expect of bishops: even more than the parish clergy they are expected to be masters of a huge variety of roles – pastor, CEO, committee chairman, visionary leader, problem solver, facilitator, administrator, team leader, preacher, conference speaker, international trouble-shooter etc. No bishop can fulfil all these roles effectively, especially in large diocese.

Bishops, particularly in the larger dioceses, have little time to pastor or support their clergy and lay people. They need to be more focused in their time-management, and delegate many of their endless committees. They need more time for themselves to recharge their own batteries. The days of them being addressed as 'My Lord' are, thankfully, largely over. But something of that establishment mentality does linger in the air.

There is a good case to be made for making bishops less important, downsizing their responsibilities to something akin to a rural dean. As in ancient Ireland, the bishop would be locally based, perhaps not in a monastery, but maybe in a smaller parish from which he or she would have the time to fulfil his or her Episcopal role in a more pastoral manner, while the financial and administrative issues could be dealt with entirely separately by an administrative office whose job would not be confused with that of bishop. Fixed terms, as for American presidents, would be a very good idea.

Clerical

There is a strong tendency in both our churches to be priest-centred, for the clergy to play an over-dominant role. Within the Anglican tradition this is somewhat tempered by our democratic structures; within the Roman Catholic tradition it can seriously over-stretch clergy to the point of burn out. In both traditions there is the assumption that the clergy are trained, full-time professionals who are therefore best entrusted with the mysteries of faith and the day-to-day running of church affairs. To too many the clergy *are* the Church. This assumption can drain the laity of initiative and the clergy of vigour. It can make the clergy into a rather introspective and self-serving clique. It is an assumption that has allowed clergy to get away with too much for too long: men of God were above criticism. Look where that has left us. It is increasingly obvious that it is not just the professionals who can transmit the things of God.

Busyness

Not unrelated to this is a growing cult of 'busy-ness' whereby churches generally, and clergy frequently, seem to equate spiritual life with high levels of activity – courses, programmes, house groups, prayer groups, conferences missions, events and so on. This counter-productively falls into the secular delusion that activity is more important than presence. Our world is hassled enough without the Church adding to the pressure of people's already busy lives. We need to offer alternative models, and not just try to beat the secular world at its own game.

Of course there has to be some activity: the incarnational model must not become an excuse for laziness. Balance is needed: too much activity, as well as too little, can be no more than a different manifestation of the same underlying introspection that interprets everything in narrow, 'churchy' terms. The incarnational model involves *being*, and being necessarily involves at least some activity. It is the level and type of activity that needs to be carefully discerned in response both to the gospel imperative and the local situation – carefully being the operative word. We do not have to be doing 'religious' or 'churchy' things to be witnesses to Christ. Indeed, the gospel might become more transparent if we were less outwardly religious. 'Piety' and 'enthusiasm' can be deeply off-putting.

Comfortable and unchallenging

However, the Church, by and large, can be comfortable and unchallenging. People need comfort but they also need to be challenged. Many have become oblivious to social challenge in the teaching of Jesus and the Bible as a whole. Even Catholic Social teaching which, in recent years especially, has been profoundly challenging, is often couched in such careful committee-speak that its true impact is lost on any but the most attentive reader.

'Comfortable', with God as our comforter, can also be banal. With this comfortable God, in our comfortable community of like-minded people, we tend to stay with our own, never moving beyond our comfort-zone. This very natural tendency was evident during our 'Troubles' in Northern Ireland, when it took a long time for the Churches generally to act as more than chaplains to their respective communities, massaging their hurts and sense of righteous victimhood. We need comfort but as a base from which to venture forth, not as a hidey-hole. We need to move beyond the image of the God-who-mends-our-brokenness to the God-who-offers-us-life-in-all-its-fullness and sends us out into the world to share that new life with all and sundry.

There was a time, not long past, in which both our Churches (and the wider Church community in Ireland) preached hell-fire and damnation, seeking to scare people into the Kingdom of Love. Heaney's vision is one that was not unique to Catholic rural Ulster:

> *'...I heard a shout*
> *As an El Greco ascetic rose before me*
> *Preaching hellfire, Saurian and stormy,*
> *Adze-head on the rampage in the pulpit.*
>
> *...Which 'put the wind up me and my generation'[8].*

And Derek Mahon's critique of his north Belfast Anglican upbringing in which a 'God-fearing, God-chosen purist little puritan' could only 'speak with a bleak afflatus' without understanding or forgiveness[9], would not have been alien to Heaney either.

Establishment

Speaking from within the Anglican tradition, and as one whose personal background is very establishment, I have to agree with Brian's comment below that one of our main weaknesses is the perception of establishment. I say perception because since 1869 we have not been the established Church.

In the recent past our Churches held a privileged place in Irish society, both in the North and in the Republic. Clergy were on the platform at public events, invited to speak on radio and TV, acted as school and hospital governors and were generally assumed to have something intelligent to say on almost any topic. They were listened to with respect. That is the ethos within which both of us began our ministry. Now that respect has, rightly, to be earned.

Things changed as the general population became painfully aware that this position of privilege was frequently abused. But the assumptions behind this unthinking acceptance of privilege have still not gone away. Churches in Northern Ireland, especially the two that are the focus of this book, still too often work with an establishment mentality, albeit one expressed in different ways according to context.

In the USA, Churches are very different from Ireland. With the growth of ecumenism they have had to compete with each other: if members do not like one Church it is much easier to change allegiance than would have been the case in the past in Ireland. In the USA Churches also play a different role than those in Ireland because the USA is a superpower. They need to work out ways to critique the massively strong political power of the federal government, and also to deal with the myriad of justice issues that come up within each state in areas such as welfare, nuclear disarmament, economic and environmental policy of global significance, war and abortion.

The USA is a highly religious society in comparison with most of Europe, and increasingly so with Ireland. That is both a positive and a negative: positive, because at least initially many are willing to listen to Churches; negative, because there can be a hidden assumption that this willingness to listen depends on Churches not challenging the establishment too much.

We still carry with us some of the habits of establishment. Our structures copy those of the established Church of England and, although our bishops are not members of the House of Lords, it is almost inevitable that they be viewed by outsiders as though they were (the acceptance, while he was still in office, by the former Archbishop of Armagh, Robin Eames, of a life peerage was seen by many as unhelpful in this regard).

Members of denominations who were on the receiving end of the penal laws have the Anglican alliance with the colonial authorities firmly embedded in their psyche, whatever the contemporary reality. It is hard to know how to shift this perception, subliminal though it is.

The Church of Ireland is democratic, but it does not always feel that way. Members of the Diocesan Synod are elected by the parishes and so voters know the people for whom they are voting. But when members of the Diocesan Synod vote for candidates for offices within the diocese and the wider Church they frequently do not know them at all. This is perhaps reflected in the difficulty many dioceses have in getting enough people to allow their names to go forward in the first place. This is a particular problem in larger dioceses. Furthermore, since the General Synod meets for several days during the week it consists largely of retired people or those who can afford to take a few days off mid-week. In other words, it is largely elderly and middle class. For all the merits of those so elected, this means that General Synod is only marginally representative, and has a limited understanding of life on the margins – a bit like parliament, in fact.

In its attempt to move away from an establishment model, the Church has increasingly organised itself in a corporate model, with a significant central and diocesan bureaucracy. This results in cost/benefit analyses and data-driven decisions, which in their turn lead to a corporatist decision-making process where bums-on-pews are the most important criterion. The complex reality of human spirituality and need is forgotten in a fixation with numbers. The Church becomes a company, the bishop the CEO and the rector little more than an area sales manager. Time with people gets pushed to the margins. Such bureaucracy costs money, and its benefits are often lost on the parishes, particularly the smaller parishes.

Divisions

The Church of Ireland is also becoming increasingly divided. Not too long ago we could justifiably be accused of being a bit bland, with all our clergy trained at the same institution in Dublin. Now many of our clergy are trained elsewhere, and many are coming to Ireland from other provinces of the Anglican Communion. Generally this is a breath of fresh air, but in some cases it has brought with it hints of the Evangelical/Catholic, High Church/Low Church divisions apparent in the provinces from which they have come. This is destructive both of unity and of charity. Some dioceses have become cold places for people of other traditions within Anglicanism. There are also alarming hints of a North/South divide within the Irish Church, with the North tending to the Evangelical and the South to the liberal. This is deeply unhelpful.

Liturgy

Anglican liturgy is one of the Church's glories and strengths, but it can become a millstone. Unimaginatively celebrated it can become routine and dull, a fact that has led some churches, particularly those of a more evangelical/charismatic persuasion, to dispense entirely with the set liturgy. This has the effect of cutting the Church loose from its moorings and from that sense of rootedness that is so important for a rounded spirituality. Churches that follow this path offer the same thing as countless other Methodist, Presbyterian, Baptist or Congregationalist Churches. While not bad in itself, this means that there is nothing distinctively *Anglican* in what is offered. Our roots are important, not just in terms of the style of worship they encourage us to offer, but also and more importantly in terms of how they nurture our spirituality and our approach to God. At its heart Anglicanism is both Catholic and reformed, and is an important bridge in a divided ecclesiastical world. We cannot afford to lose either strand: if we do we will wither away in the pursuit of short term, statistically driven and, ultimately, illusory gains.

Physical dominance

In Ireland churches are very dominant, at least physically. This is, in part, a reflection of the days when the Churches were also socially dominant, and churches were built as a public statement of that dominance. Sometimes denominations competed with each other to have the largest and most splendid building in the neighbourhood. This gives an impression of wealth and privilege. Although today many churches are struggling financially the impression given is one of genteel prosperity, with clergy in houses considerably better than they could afford if paying for themselves. This appearance of wealth gives off a damaging first impression.

One of the unintended side effects of this 'establishment model' is that things of faith have become blended into the routine of life. At its best this is exactly what the Church should be encouraging, creating a seamless robe of lived faith amongst her people. Too often, however, the things of faith become routine and formal; we get dosed with just enough Christianity to ensure that we don't catch the real thing.

Establishment has also been a very local thing. Being embedded in the local community the Church has tended to reflect local attitudes, opinions and divisions. Happy in its comfort zone the Church members all too rarely challenge each other, even when their values are hard to square with the gospel. We are afraid of losing local support, or of offending people and losing them (and their financial contributions). This is psychologically and sociologically understandable, but not gospel-based.

Both of us have found that this understandable fear was sometimes unnecessary. Each of us has tackled controversial issues in the pulpit, half afraid that a walkout would ensue. Yet, there have been no walkouts.

In some cases, the reaction has been gratitude that hard topics have been wrestled with and that the values of our faith have been brought to bear upon the thorny issues of our day. Not everyone has agreed with our analyses, but they have found the questions liberating: they made faith relevant. At other times, some have rejected the message while accepting that preaching peace is something clergy should be doing, the implication being that this does not apply in the 'real' world.

Signs of life

Within the Church of Ireland there is also much life: there is faithful witness Sunday by Sunday throughout the year, and there is pastoral sensitivity from both clergy and lay people. There are many examples of parishes imaginatively tackling local issues such as deprivation and sectarianism, with others tackling environmental issues with enthusiasm and vision, and yet others seeking to deepen their spiritual life through courses such as Alpha and Emmaus. This liveliness goes beyond the dioceses: at a more centralised level initiatives such as that of the Hard Gospel Project, an initiative focused on sectarianism and which we will discuss later, have made a significant contribution to the national debate.

Yet these things tend to be of minority interest: most Church members are unaware of the Hard Gospel Project and many would run a mile at the thought of an Alpha course. It can be hard to reconcile the Church of the activist and the church-in-the-pew. It takes time for the insights gained to filter down.

The Church of Ireland shares with the Roman Catholic Church the huge richness of the sacraments, especially the Eucharist – shared theologically, but regrettably not often in practice – our spirituality, and the vast works of justice done by members of the Churches in Ireland and abroad. We have all been given the extraordinary gift of knowing Christ Jesus, his Father and the Holy Spirit. Yet so much of this richness will not come to full fruition unless we face radical reform. Unfortunately, but perhaps inevitably, most attempts at reform are haphazard, individualistic and geographically uneven.

A real process of prayerful discernment needs to take place, as is being done to some extent in the case of the Church's consideration of human sexuality. One of the results of this has been a more respectful listening and more mature discussion. This was evident in the difference between the tone of the debates at the 2013 and 2014 General Synods in Ireland. In the first debate there was real tension, dogmatism, even hostility and recrimination. In the second there was a respectful listening, which was perhaps symbolised best by the warmth of the reception for the Dean of Leighlin, who is in a civil partnership. People stepped back from the brink and, even though real divisions remained, the integrity of all participants was beginning to be recognised and respected.

Anglicanism can become vague. While the Anglican *via media* is a model I hold dear, it can become a wishy-washy, all-things-to-all-men-and-women sort of approach. The middle ground is not an easy place to be, and to articulate and defend it with clarity can be hard. Yet, it needs to be done, or else we will come to be seen as folk who lack conviction.

The Anglican Communion
The Church of Ireland is, of course, part of the wider Anglican Communion, a fellowship of thirty-nine provinces from places as diverse as the USA, Nigeria, Scotland, Japan, Melanesia and Korea. This has the potential for great richness, a diversity in which we learn from each other through both our agreements and our differences. However, in recent years this diversity has been stretched to the limit, to the extent that many in the media are predicting the imminent breakup of the Anglican Communion – something that was only

narrowly, and controversially, avoided in January 2016.

At the heart of these tensions are different approaches to Scripture – not the specific issues of human sexuality and women bishops that often hog the headlines. The Churches of the Global South, along with parts of the American Church and others, place great emphasis on a literal interpretation of Scripture and therefore find the liberal thrust of the majority of the Communion to be almost heretical. It will be fairly obvious, even to the most casual reader of these pages, where I sit in this debate. The fault for this is far from being one sided, and the apportioning of blame, although tempting, is unhelpful. All sides in the debate have fallen short of the glory of God, and all have resorted to a dogmatism that is alien to Anglican history and tradition; all have fallen into the trap of believing that there is only one 'right' in these matters, and all have forgotten that God, and the things of God, are bigger than our limited capacity to understand. We all have a limited and partial grasp of where truth lies.

An exchange on the Australian blogosphere concerning a recent Episcopal election stated that 'we need to be ready to stand with our brothers and sisters who want to stand for truth in the face of error.' The same language is often heard emanating from parts of the African Church. The world is reduced to a very un-Anglican black and white, with no shading or colour. The impression is gained that it is not Christ who matters, but rather our own cherished doctrines, in which we are always right and those who nuance things differently, wrong. This is tragic and deeply un-evangelical.

The 'liberal wing' of the Communion can be equally intolerant however, and often in a condescending sort of way, looking down their noses at the simpletons on the other side, who lack intellectual depth or spiritual warmth. This liberal wing can appear patronising, and this patronising attitude can be destructive: it can give the impression that they, those of the 'liberal wing', alone are the guardians of truth. Both sides tend to forget that in Christianity, truth is a person, word become flesh: truth can never be limited to a set of verbal propositions..

Fortunately, this is not all that there is. To many − if not most − in the pews such debates seem arcane at best, uncharitable at worst. They are more concerned with exploring and living their faith. They want to be stretched, excited, challenged and warmed by what the Church has to offer. They are a silent majority whose silence, I pray, may prove louder than the party-ecclesiastical spokesmen and women whose siren voices are so loved by the media.

Elsewhere I have referred to the benefit of stepping back a bit and learning to listen − as in the case of the debate on human sexuality. Yet this 'stepping back' is not always apparent, and as a result there is a climate of recrimination and complacency that is contrary to all that I hold dear. Justin Welby, the Archbishop of Canterbury, has his work cut out in maintaining our cherished unity in diversity.

Response (Brian Lennon)

The Church of Ireland looks very attractive to many in the Roman Catholic Church, and many have left to join it. There is a vast commonality of doctrine and liturgy. The Eucharistic service is almost indistinguishable. Structures are much more democratic, with an authentic voice given to lay people. Further, the Anglican Communion as a whole deals openly with a range of issues that are debated hotly within the Roman Church, such as the ordination of women and the status of homosexual relationships. The difference is that where Anglicans have much publicised disputes, debates and well-ordered procedures, Roman Catholics were, until recently, officially banned from even discussing some of these issues, for example the ordination of women.

In practice Pope Francis has softened this, for example his comment on gay people 'who am I to judge?', a comment which, while it shows no change in the teaching of the official Church on this issue, marks the beginning of a journey towards treating people with proper respect. This is a journey that is likely in its turn to lead to more open discussion about the validity of current Church teaching.

It is precisely because of the processes available to Anglicans, and the positions which they have reached on some of these issues through use of those processes, that some Roman Catholics have changed denomination.

Traditionally, the divisions between our two Churches focused on the powers of the papacy. There was much to justify Henry VIII's refusal to accept the papacy's rejection of his divorce: arguably the issue was primarily political. Henry's initial break, however, motivated as it was by divorce, was followed by deeper Elizabethan reforms. This introduced a gulf between our Churches that continues today. The work of ecumenists over the past 100 years has helped reduce it. It is important to note that participants in these dialogues have reached agreement on baptism, ministry, Eucharist and even the role of the papacy. These agreements have not, however, been accepted by the wider Church, and the Roman Catholic Church has arguably been the biggest block in this regard.

Three issues are particularly important. One is the role of the papacy. We both believe that the papacy needs reform. At the very least this reform would include greater involvement of local churches, and of lay people, in decisions about all aspects of Church life, including doctrine, as was the case for the first millennium of the Church's existence.

For most part, the ordination of women, including women bishops, officially seems to have been resolved as an issue in much of the Anglican Communion. The Church of Ireland was ahead of Britain in ordaining Pat Storey as Bishop of Meath and Kildare. Many Roman Catholic commentators, including as committed an ecumenist as Cardinal Kasper, have argued that women's ordination has widened the gulf with the Roman Church, because the latter can never follow suit. For both of us the thesis that God is for all times and in all circumstances absolutely opposed to the ordination of women remains incomprehensible, other than in terms of patriarchy.

I agree with the paradox highlighted by Tim: relying on the papacy as the main element in the reform of the papacy gives the papacy too much power. Yet, paradoxically, an absolute monarchy can only be reformed by its absolute monarch – unless it is to be abolished. There are scriptural arguments for a primacy, and historical arguments for it being centred in Rome. None of these exclude a variety of options, and the way primacy has been exercised has varied considerably throughout history. For the first millennium, its world-wide influence was very limited and this changed only gradually throughout the second millennium. At the beginning of the nineteenth century less than twenty-five per cent of bishops were appointed by Rome. Rome's centralising ecclesial power grew in conjunction with the decline of the political power of the Papal States from the mid-nineteenth century. In recent decades both John Paul II and Francis have made strong pleas for its reform. Rome has an important role to play as a symbol of unity for the universal church. The papacy in collegial union with bishops could exercise an authority greater than that of Lambeth conferences, and one that arguably is needed. Such effective symbols of unity and of appropriately collegial authority are needed all the more as the increasing diversity of human beings is recognised, although this authority may well be in tension with Anglican instincts. Those instincts are important. So too is the Roman instinct for unity. Both churches need each other in order to reform the papacy: the Roman Church with its emphasis on unity and authority; the Church of Ireland with its collegial emphasis. Without both these gifts we will end up with our status quo: a Roman Church where, legally, absolute authority is vested in the papacy, albeit often ignored, and an Anglican Communion, where it can sometimes be difficult to see the difference between polite disagreement and basic schism: how can a woman bishop effectively exercise her charism in her diocese if members of the Church do not recognise her authority in practice? Is this disagreement or schism?

Theoretically the Roman Church still does not recognise the ordination of Anglicans. So, I am a priest, Tim, officially, a lay person. That is not a view either of us supports. But there is still a considerable way to go for the Roman Church to bring its theology and law into harmony with the long experience of so many of its members who accept the validity of Anglican orders in practice.

A weakness in the Church of Ireland is its historical links with the establishment. This is most striking in the military paraphernalia displayed in many churches. The issue in part is about memory: people should remember their loved ones who died in wars. The problem is that it is nearly always only one side that is remembered: *ours*. The enemies they fought, whom they killed and at whose hands they died, are invisible. So also is any critique of what the church's loved ones did: were all the wars in which they took part just and unavoidable? Were all their actions within these wars just? Even if they were, where is the awareness of the enemy, whom Christ calls us to love? The focus on reconciliation in a Cathedral like Canterbury is a challenge to the Communion as a whole to examine in what way they are tied into militarism, and to an uncritical support of the state.

The Church of Ireland is also open to the charge of being more of a middle- and upper-class Church and having too little involvement with the working-class. Some individual congregations manage to buck this trend. This is also an issue for all Churches, and increasingly so for the Roman Catholic Church. We will deal with some of the reasons for this in the next chapter.

Chapter 8: Issues Facing Both Our Churches

Diversity and outcasts

Jesus as a human being had to learn about diversity. As we have seen, he built close and public relationships with outcasts. In this he was following his own Jewish tradition:

> 'You will not molest or oppress aliens, for you yourselves were once aliens in Egypt. You will not ill-treat widows or orphans; if you ill-treat them in any way and they make an appeal to me for help, I shall certainly hear their appeal, my anger will be roused and I shall put you to the sword; then your own wives will be widows, and your own children orphans' (*Ex.22:20-24*).

One of the great examples of Jesus learning about diversity is in his encounter with the – nameless – Caananite woman (*Mt.15*). The woman is desperate to find a cure for her daughter but Jesus will not respond to her because he came only for the people of Israel. The woman humiliates herself by arguing that even the dogs at the table eat the food that falls from the children's table. Only at that point does Jesus respond.

In this encounter Jesus, as a Jewish human being, limited by his own culture and context, learns from a woman and a foreigner that God's good news is for all. The Kingdom of God is also to some extent a gift rather than an impossible ideal, something that is among us both as potential and reality. It is something that happens, most particularly in the person of Jesus, but also in and through those who seek to follow him, and among others; it is something that is dynamic, interpersonal and challenging. The Christian is called to live within that kingdom, and also to bring it about. It is already here, but its current reality is to some extent dependent on our willingness to live by it.

This text may also be an echo of the vision in Isaiah chapter 60 and elsewhere in the Old Testament that the Gentiles would in time come to the feast of Yahweh.

Like our Master, we too, need to learn about diversity.

For our Churches to be witnesses to Christ we have to show the same reaching out to outcasts and sinners that Jesus did, but always with the knowledge that we too are sinners.

In the light of this none of our Churches are diverse enough, and where there appears to be diversity it all too often descends into acrimonious partisanship. This is also true of many Churches internationally. It was striking that, during the Troubles in Northern Ireland, when Protestant and Catholic clergy were invited to the USA, our hosts were shocked at our divisions, but the only visible colour of people in most of the churches that we visited was white.

We need to be realistic: we can only be as diverse as the population among whom we live. Yet diversity in Northern Ireland has increased dramatically in recent years, so if our Churches are not diverse why is this? Are there ways we can change our worship to attract people of different background or ethnicity from our current congregation? Do we look for outsiders to join? Do we think about our culture: all the different things we never question, but which to an outsider may look quite strange?

There are specific issues for the Catholic Church in this area. The Church under John Paul II and Benedict XVI was vehement in its condemnation of active lesbian, gay, bisexual and transgender people, and Benedict as Cardinal Ratzinger and as Prefect of the Congregation for the Doctrine of the Faith saw homosexuality as something 'intrinsically disordered'.[10]

Pope Francis softened the harshness of this condemnation with a question asked early in his papal ministry: 'who am I to judge them?'

That question suggests that we can never condemn a *person*, however much we may disagree with his or her morality. Nor can we be self-righteous. The issue was hotly debated at the Synods on the Family in October 2014 and 2015. Secular society in the West has changed dramatically in its moral evaluation of this issue in the past twenty years. This change has happened among people from all backgrounds, ages and religions. Those who approve state acceptance of LGBT relationships are now in the majority. Given the dramatic nature of this change in secular society, changes in the way the Church responds to these relationships cannot be ruled out.

Something that was referred to in the communiqués that followed the Anglican Primates' meeting of January 2016 is important here. David Chillingworth, bishop of St Andrew's and Primus of the Scottish Episcopal Church, made the valid point that 'African provinces suffer missional cost because they are associated with the US Episcopal Church through the Anglican Communion. Assertive Islam, moving through Africa, can portray them as a "gay Church". More liberal churches can be accused of homophobia, because they are associated with conservative African provinces through the Communion. There, too, a missional cost is paid, particularly in our work among young people.' It is a hard circle to square. What may be accepted in the USA or Ireland can be deeply problematical in Kenya or Nigeria.

Two aspects of the issue need to be kept separate: respect for persons, and doctrinal disputes. Members of both our Churches are divided on doctrinal issues, but there can be no disagreement about the need to respect persons. Further, when people's sexual orientation is officially condemned they are likely to experience the Church as a cold place.

The first question for diversity then is: is our Church welcoming to LGBT people or not? The only people who can authoritatively answer this are LGBT people themselves. There are many LGBT people who accept conservative Church teaching, so our first question needs to be: do we have openly LGBT people as members of our Church structures and committees?

The same question needs to be raised about people born in other countries: are they in positions of influence in our Church or not? If not, how can we know that we are taking on the demands of diversity in our worship, celebration or service?

Diversity needs to be shown in other ways. Given the bias against women among many, we need to make sure that the majority of our decision-making bodies include a significant number of women. That should be easy: far more women than men attend and are active in our churches, but it is often the men who end up in leadership roles, even apart from clerical ones (conversely, in some Church of Ireland parishes today, the Select Vestry is heavily female-represented).

There is a danger that men opt out when women become better represented, and that the Church moves from being over-patriarchal to being female dominated but still working within patriarchal structures and assumptions. And, as we have frequently mentioned, working class people and the unemployed are under-represented. Changing that will not be easy, but it needs to be done.

Jesus was not a great organiser. He developed a vision of how human beings should live in order to become fully human. Vast numbers followed him in the early days. But opposition grew from religious and political leaders whose position was threatened. In the end almost all his followers deserted him. He died a criminal, in a death seen as shameful in his own Jewish scriptures. The movement he founded was riven by conflict from the beginning – the Churches in Corinth, Galatia and Ephesus, to which Paul wrote in trenchant terms, were all split into vigorous factions. We cannot expect our Church to be different in this respect. Indeed, as we have mentioned several times, if there was not conflict, within and between our Churches, we would not be the Church: we would be a group of like-minded people.

Conflict, in itself, is no bad thing: the way we deal with it can be. Dealing with it constructively can challenge complacency and help us to understand those from whom we differ and their motives. We can learn to respect others, especially when we are absolutely opposed to their beliefs. That is why *process* is at least as important as outcome. A majority vote that reaches a correct decision is not Christian if it does so in a way that disrespects the minority.

The difference between the dialogue within the Church of Ireland Synods in 2013 and in 2014, as noted above by Tim, was due to prayerful discernment. That is a critical element in the difference between disagreement and Christian disagreement.

Healing, repentance, forgiving and prayer

Healing takes many forms. One comes from inclusion, respect and recognition. How much has the fall away from attendance in the Catholic Church, for example, been due to many feeling invisible in the Church? In a short survey on attitudes to the Church by the Justice and Peace Commission of the Armagh Roman Catholic diocese in 2013 it was striking how many people said that they appreciated being consulted. They saw the survey as taking them seriously and recognising them as members. It is easier for Protestant than Catholic Church members to feel a sense of belonging to and recognition by the Church simply because congregations are often smaller. This means that we need a new ministry in the Catholic Church: parish visitors, who are trained, who visit parishioners on behalf of the parish, and who are able to report back to the people they visit about actions that have been taken in response to concerns they have raised.

Within both our Churches there is much hope, especially at the local, parochial, level. People often display a deep understanding of kingdom values both in their own personal lives and in the way they relate to the wider community. There is often a real selflessness within Church communities, one that challenges the egocentricity of the world around us. There is a real expression (although not one that would be expressed in these terms) of faith lived *out there*, in the community, without necessarily having a 'Christian' or 'Church' label attached to it. That is good as it shows that the message is getting through. It is perhaps all the stronger in that it hasn't been owned, institutionalised or labelled by the institutional Church.

Other signs of life

There are many other signs of life in the Irish Churches: within the Catholic Church over 800,000 people visit Knock annually, 8,000 visit Lough Derg and huge numbers visit Lourdes, including an army of volunteers – many young – who look after invalids. Redemptorist retreats – with lay people as part of the retreat team – pack churches North and South for as many as ten sessions a day. The annual Clonard Novena in Belfast is noteworthy because of the strong input from clergy from other Churches. A large number of people have made the Ignatian exercises a part of their daily life. Monasteries like the Cistercians in Glenstal and Rostrevor, and the Cistercians in Mount Melleray welcome visitors from many different denominational backgrounds. There are a large number of prayer groups throughout the country.

The Conference of Religious of Ireland and the Society of Vincent de Paul raise serious questions about injustice. The new structures in

Armagh and other dioceses have involved many lay people in Church decisions and there are an increasing number of lay people with theological degrees.

Ecumenism

Ecumenism has made progress in Ireland. Gone are the days when clergy groups engaged in genteel discussions about the psalms while the Troubles in Northern Ireland raged outside the room. There now tends to be much more honesty, humility, respect, a willingness to learn from each other and genuine friendship. But we continue to have separate Churches despite Our Lord's desire that we should be one (*Jn.17*). In some places, ecumenical relationships are still confined to Church Unity Octave, and occasional joint study groups, especially in Lent and Advent. The first joint service for Church Unity Octave was held in one town in Northern Ireland as recently as 2014.

There are some outstanding exceptions to this: clergy have often come together to celebrate the appointment of a new leader of another denomination, and there have been many examples of joint support in the face of the terrible atrocities of the Troubles; chaplains from different denominations work well together in prisons and hospitals, while the Clonard Mission is an extraordinary example of clergy from many different Churches preaching together; and the Faith and Politics Group was an explicit effort by Christians from different denominations to reflect together on the Troubles. Churches often cooperate well on third-world issues and places like Corrymeela are examples of joint Christian witness to peace making. Nonetheless, ecumenism does not often impinge on the ordinary Sunday worship of our Churches.

An obvious way to do this is by sharing preachers. This, of course, raises fears but these fears need to be confronted. One is doctrinal: how can we be sure that the preacher will be theologically correct?

The answer is by using the same standards that we use within our denominations. In the Roman Catholic Church this means ensuring people pass theological exams before ordination. Further, having Protestant clergy preach in Catholic churches will surely increase the theological knowledge of our priests, and raise new questions which can lead to further learning. In reality it may be more difficult for Church of Ireland congregations to share pulpits, so in some places the exchange may work one way, and not the other. So be it! At least Roman Catholics will gain from hearing Protestant clergy, and such exchanges may gradually affect other Churches.

A second issue is logistical: many Sunday services take place at the same time. So it may be that the time of one or both services may have to be changed on some days. Any priest or minister knows the difficulties this will raise. The question then needs to be asked: how much does it matter that we continue to be separate Churches, when this is clearly something that pains Our Lord? Is our worship simply to fulfil ourselves, or is it to worship God? If it is the latter, then we need to ask what God wants. Even without changing the times of services and Mass, retired clergy could be asked to preach, but clearly this is less satisfactory than bringing together currently active clergy.

Other initiatives are easier: lay readers, shared choirs, joint announcements of initiatives to serve in the area of justice, and so on. People now are far more relaxed about other denominations than they were forty years ago. They are more willing to listen to people of different backgrounds and traditions, to pray for them when they are going through turbulent times and to pray with them when the opportunity arises. Old brick walls are being dissolved.

Spreading and discovering the word

'Evangelisation' is often seen as a major task of the Church. Both of us are wary of it, at least in its popular understanding. It means to preach the gospel, or to seek converts. Why should we be uneasy about this? Is it not for this that we were baptised, confirmed and ordained?

Within Northern Ireland, perhaps more so in the Protestant than in the Catholic community, preachers preach the gospel in public and hand out gospel tracts. For us, however, what is crucial is *how* we approach the task of spreading the good news. It is critically important that we do so in a way that respects those we meet. We Christians do not have all the answers. We have an experience, an extraordinary one, of encountering Christ. At the heart of that is mystery: in a real sense we do not know what it is about. We do know, however, that our relationship with Christ has given incredible meaning to our own lives, and also given us a way to approach life, suffering and death.

There is nothing in this experience which necessitates our foisting this package on to other people. We do not fully know Christ: we have been graced to experience only the tiniest element of him. Others, if they come to know Christ, will certainly do so in a way different from us, and this will have its own richness. This means that dialogue is at the heart of spreading the word, and for dialogue to take place a number of things need to be in place. One is respect for others. This has nothing to do with agreement. Indeed, one of the conditions for dialogue is that we *disagree*. If we agree about everything we will have nothing to learn from each other. Respect is about recognising that we can learn from the other. In particular it means that we listen deeply so that we hear the other person's story: the people and experiences that really have mattered in his or her life.

We can and should come to dialogue with our own strong, and sometimes non-negotiable, views. There are many, many things about which neither of us are open to change: the fact that Jesus is one with God, that God is one and yet three, that Jesus became fully human, that the Church, with all its corruption, is essential for Christians, and in the moral order, for example, that the death penalty is always wrong. Dialogue about any of these issues is not for us about being open to an ultimate change. In dialogue we can learn much about the meaning of quite mysterious faith statements. That is why, for example, Christian–Jewish dialogue is so important for Christian theology – just as it can be for Jewish self-understanding. For Christians there is a particular reason why this dialogue is so important: our Saviour was Jewish, albeit coming from a tradition likely to differ considerably from that of Jewish people we meet today. Judaism, no less than Christianity, is diverse, and has changed throughout history. So Christians and Jewish people can talk, listen and seek to understand each other, and in the process learn much about their own as well as the others' faith, without seeking to convert each other. Indeed, starting with the notion of conversion can be disrespectful to our dialogue partner: there is an assumption that I have something that you need, namely Christ, and that you need to know and experience Christ *in the same way* that I do. That is the trap: dialogue in that context moves swiftly from a respectful encounter into an egotistic attempt to impose our experience on someone else. We can be certain – if we are Christians – that others need Christ. We can be almost certain that they will experience Christ in a *different way from us*. Certainty, as we have suggested earlier, puts a stop to creative dialogue.

We want to introduce people to Christ, the Christian tradition and the Christian message. First, however, we need to hear their story, their experience, their understanding of the world. Christ, when he met the woman from Samaria at the well (*Jn. 4*) did not start by preaching to her that she needed to give up her Samaritan beliefs and accept his Jewish beliefs. Instead he asked her for water. There is a concrete humanity in this. Doing so was startling: he was

Jewish and he was asking a Samaritan, the enemies of the Jewish people, for water. He was a man speaking to a strange woman. He was therefore operating outside his own culture and conventions. As the story moves forward he points out that the man with whom the woman is living is not her husband (this is likely an analogy for the covenant between God and Jews, and a way to suggest that Samaritans have separated themselves from it). Yet, Jesus does not continue to focus on this. He does not make sorting out her marital situation, or her conversion to Judaism, a condition of continuing the dialogue. Instead he offers her the water of eternal life. The woman responds, believes, becomes a missionary and tells the rest of the village about him. They come and see. They encounter him. Finally they believe, not simply because of her witness, but because they have experienced Christ themselves. At the end of the story there is no indication that they all have to stop being Samaritans but they will face questions as to how to do this and, at the same time, accept Christ as their Saviour.

That story is a model of how to spread the good news about Christ. Focus on people's real needs: in the woman's case, water; show respect – even if her marital or faith position was 'disordered'; and be willing to go beyond enmity and convention. This focus on her real needs leads to a surprising outcome: she lets others know about her experience, and finally the whole village comes to belief through their own encounter with Christ. In this exchange there is dialogue, respect, searching, mystery and surprise. This process is the complete opposite of one that presents people with a package and tells them that they have to accept it in order to be saved.

So what concrete measures do we need in the Church to encourage people to be open to experience Christ? Here we are thinking of the institutional Church. It may be useful to think of three fairly distinct groups: the first are regular church goers, the a second are people who connect with the church for births, marriages and deaths, but rarely on other occasions, and the third are the un-churched: they might attend church for social reasons, but they are either atheists or more likely, agnostics.

The first group, the church goers, above all others must not be taken for granted by clergy and other Church leaders. In the Roman Catholic Church they, like most people, have been deeply scandalised by the abuse of children. They feel the pain of belonging to a Church that has often earned its terrible press. They resent the absence of public comment about the rich spirituality and service of the Church, and they have refused to be separated from the Church because of the sins of some leaders. Their faith is not dependent on the morality of clergy. They experience a real connection between the Eucharist, the other sacraments and their daily life. They pray and have a personal experience of Christ. Some are increasingly taking up leadership positions in the Church and seeking out theological education. They make up their own minds about Church teaching and will sometimes not accept it. Above all they need encouragement. They also need clergy who facilitate rather than rule them. It is from this group that many leaders of the Church will come. If the Church is to reach out to non-church goers, it will be through this group or not at all. It is with this group that theological education needs to be continued and increased in the first instance. They also need to be involved in renewing and developing the liturgy.

It should not be assumed that all regular church goers think the same. Some accept the Church's teaching on all issues. Others ignore it. Still others actively oppose it. If the latter are lay people the Church will often take no action against them (unless they are in jobs such as teaching). If they are priests or other clergy they may be censored or banned from preaching, or excommunicated. This is especially true of the Roman Catholic Church, but has also happened within the Church of Ireland.

The second group, whose contact with the church is mainly through births, marriages and deaths, is large. Some have given up regular attendance because of the abuse scandals, others because their previous attendance was mainly due to social conformity and the need for this has greatly decreased.

Positive results can be obtained by treating people seriously and with respect. This involves not only listening to people, but also responding to what they have to say. This does not mean always accepting their proposals, but people should be told after they have been consulted what the response of the Church is and why this response has been given. Taking people seriously, moreover, means giving them a role in actual decision making, depending on their level of involvement with the Church.

The Presbyterian model of having a dedicated team of people in every parish or cluster to visit every home on a regular basis has much to recommend it. This is probably the best way to make a personal link between the parish and individuals, although it can become rather formalised. The purpose of such visits, however, should not be to get people back to Church. Rather, it should be about building pastoral relationships; relationships that in turn that could lead to conversations about spirituality, possible retreats or other spiritual exercises, or engagement in justice projects and this could open up discussions about faith education and practice.

The third group contains many with almost no feelings about the Church – it simply does not appear on their horizon – as well as others who are deeply opposed to the Church. It is really important that the Church finds ways to engage with people in this group. This is as much for the Church's own benefit as theirs. Otherwise we end up talking only to those sympathetic to the Church and miss out on the insights of others. It is also important that the Church insists on having an appropriate place in the public media. This is not on the basis of any special pleading, but because Church members are citizens and we have as much right as others to have our voice heard. While being open to dialogue in a non-defensive way we need to oppose discrimination and false information vigorously.

A few years ago the Church of Ireland Diocese of Down and Dromore held a 'Year of Mission' in which every parish was asked to host a special mission orientated event. Many parishes chose predictable paths and had weeks of visiting speakers and lots of activity. Helen's Bay parish (of which Tim is Rector) chose a different path, largely because it was suspected that a traditional mission would be a turn-off in an area where most people are educated to a university level or above. In the Protestant community 'mission' is largely associated with tents in fields and a fundamentalist preacher telling folk what they must do to be saved. Obviously this is a stereotype, but it is one that still holds a great deal of negative power. It is not the way to approach an educated community.

Rather, it was felt that the parish should, amongst other things, hold a series of talks throughout the year, loosely entitled 'Food for Thought', in which people from non-church backgrounds, mainly in the arts, spoke of how they had been touched by God through non-church media: poetry, the visual arts, music and so on. It was an attempt to show people that they did not have to leave their mind and æsthetic sense at the door of the church, and it was an effort to reach them where they were. It is too early to say whether this approach has been successful but, at the very least, there has been a significant expression of gratitude that the Church is looking at these things in this way, a sense of relief that the old stereotypes of the Church are not necessarily true. That is one approach to evangelism, one that respects where people are.

Conclusion

Neither of us are under any illusions about the difficulty in bringing about positive change in either of our Churches. Catholics rightly call for more lay involvement. Tim points to the way this has worked out in the Church of Ireland Synod: the lay people who are involved at national level are almost all retired because people in employment cannot easily take a week off work. In both our Churches there is a strong likelihood that working class people will be under-represented. Lay people, if more are involved in governance, may make a mess of things – much as we clergy have often done. Nonetheless the arguments for lay involvement in all our Churches at a decision-making level are overwhelming: we cannot be the Church without including Church members in governance.

SECTION 3: CHURCH AND SOCIETY

Chapter 9: Why Focus on the Church and Society?

Ignatius of Loyola has a meditation early in the *Spiritual Exercises* in which he asks the retreatant to imagine the three persons of the blessed Trinity looking down on the world, seeing all the people going to hell, and choosing to send the Second Person in the Incarnation to save the world.

This imagery does not sit well with a modern audience. Nor, for us, does the idea of all going to hell. Yet, the image of the Trinity as a community of persons who want to save the world is a powerful one. It is opposed to a view that sees God as unaffected by human suffering. With due respect for the niceties of theological distinctions – and these are important – the greatest revelation of God is in Jesus Christ, and if there is one quality that stands out in his life it is surely compassion.

The call of the Church to respond to the suffering of the world is therefore not an optional extra: it is central to any individual or group who wants to follow Christ. Further, while it is obvious that Churches need to respond to individual and group suffering through the exercise of charity, it is also true that Churches need to play their part in tackling issues of structural injustice. To argue otherwise is to suggest that it is appropriate for Churches to distribute sticking plasters, but not to challenge whatever or whoever caused the injuries in the first place.

Those who say that Churches should focus on 'spiritual' issues and stay clear of social and political injustice are talking nonsense. Christ's healing, as well as his incarnation, was physical, political and social as well as spiritual.

Let us remind ourselves again of the features that we stressed in Christ's life: he was completely immersed in loving the Father and loving all people in the Father, and challenged religious and political systems that did not respect persons; he had an awareness of the need to respond to diversity, and he healed the sick; he ate and drank with outcasts and sinners, and privileged the poor; he called on all people to repent, and offered forgiveness to all, embracing suffering when that was necessary in order to stand up for compassion; he continued to trust his Father in the face of failure and death, and ultimately he was vindicated by the Father in the joy of the resurrection.

In the light of these what should the Church's priorities be? There is no simple answer: people can legitimately disagree. Further, any Church community can only do so much. We need, however, to ask about the overall impact of Church work: does it increase respect for diversity, and build solidarity – both real and perceived – in the community as a whole? Further, we need to distinguish the task of the Church overall – in which all Churches should cooperate not only with each other, but also with the appropriate secular agencies – from the role of local communities. The latter, as well as working for local change, need to contribute to the decision-making process at the macro level – something the Roman Catholic Church needs to learn from the work of Anglican and Protestant Churches on collegiality. Churches also need to do more to make visible the contribution that they make through the work of their individual members: this would encourage others to imitate them and help to make visible the contribution that Churches as a whole make to society. That is important because it bears witness to our commitment to help bring about Christ's community.

Discernment

In the early 1990s Jesuits in Central America, many of who were working in areas of deep conflict, took time out every year for a three-week long process of discernment. It is worth teasing out a little what this involved.

Discernment, as practised by these Jesuits, was not simply about thinking, much less about debating in order to win an argument. Rather, it was a process of prayer, silent reflection, discussion, listening and more prayer that was aimed at answering a question: what does the Holy Spirit want us to do in our concrete situation? The answer never comes in the form of voices from heaven. Instead it is a slowly emerging consensus that changes as members of the group grow in their freedom to listen to each other, and let go some of their own egoistic impulses. Consensus does not mean total agreement. It means that all are able to live with the decision, and also recognise that the reasons proposed for it are good. It is a process which is never perfect. Nor can it guarantee the 'best' decision. All it can do is help people make a decision that is freer of their own biases than might otherwise have been the case.

The process is based on the *Spiritual Exercises* of St Ignatius. In these, Ignatius brings the participant through a rigorous series of exercises, all designed to help people face their actual situation before God: that of being a sinner, but one loved intensely by God. Completing, at an initial level, what is involved in what has just been mentioned takes about ten days. In reality it is a life long journey that is never finished.

However, recognising our sinfulness in the face of a loving God is but one part of these exercises. The Exercises go on to invite participants to hear the call of Christ and to enter Christ's kingdom or community, a call which is central to the New Testament. In turn that raises the issue of suffering. Christ suffered precisely because he lived for God's community. Had he walked away from this community he would have walked away from suffering. That, however, would have been a rejection of love. The follower of Christ is called in the same direction: to respond to Christ' love and, if necessary, to suffer. This suffering, can take the form of repenting or forgiving. In the end, however, the Christian is also called to rejoice in the risen Lord, and rejoice not in naïve pretence that all is well in the world, but rather in a basic and deep trust that ultimately the love of God in Christ will overcome the harm we do to each other.

It is in the light of this experience of the risen Christ that Christians are asked to discern together the way forward in conflict. So what should the priorities of the Church be?

Global concerns

Our interest in the international Church is related to our personal histories. Tim found inspiration and challenge from his time in Papua New Guinea, a country of 750 languages and huge cultural variety. One of the main issues for the Church there was cross-cultural communication – how to express the gospel in terms that were comprehensible to people operating within a very different culture. Tim first went out to Papua New Guinea instinctively aware that this was an issue – perhaps that subliminal awareness was why he chose to go to a theological training institute, giving the tools to express the gospel to local people who understood the local context, rather than attempting it for himself.

In Northern Ireland that experience of Papua New Guinea was found to be formative for Tim and through Tim for Brian also, both in terms of how we have come to express our faith in today's world (first or sixteenth century concepts are not necessarily helpful in twenty-first century Ireland), but also in terms of how we have come to understand and relate to people who are different from us without either patronising or demonising them. Those questions lie behind much of what we discuss in these pages.

Ethiopia has also been a large part of Tim's life, where (during his gap-year between school and university) he worked at a school and orphanage that offered both education and a home to many of those who would otherwise have been on the streets or unable to afford any education at all. Africa had always been a part of his world-view, even though he had never actually been there. In previous generations family members had been both explorers and missionaries and a direct ancestor, Sir Thomas Fowell Buxton, had taken over the parliamentary side of the British anti-slavery movement from William Wilberforce when the latter died. That family background, and his experience of working there for himself, gave him a passion and an inspiration for both the continent and for social justice. Social justice closer to home was also part of his DNA, with both his parents being involved in various social justice issues, and with his being a direct descendant of Elizabeth Fry, the nineteenth century prison reformer whose portrait still adorns the Bank of England five pound note.

In the light of this it seems to us that at an international level the major concerns of the church should be with the environment, the economy, respect for the person as an end in him or herself, a caring concern (in Old Testament language, *hesed* or loving-kindness) for all people, giving them the tools with which to improve their own situation, and peacemaking. The integrity and safety of our planet depends on how we deal with environmental issues.

The failure to focus on the global environment is in no small part driven by that unbridled capitalism which not only caused such financial ruin in the 2008 crash but greatly increased the suffering of the poorest in our societies. That economic model is one reason for the increased number of refugees we find on the borders of Europe. Conflict over resources, affected by global environmental change, also play a role in this. As the world population grows and resources – particularly water – diminish because of environmental pressures, more people will be driven from their homes. In 2015 thousands lost their lives in desperate attempts to cross the Mediterranean to get to Europe. With no obvious resolution to conflicts in the Middle East and in some parts of Africa, this movement of peoples is almost guaranteed to increase.

A number of values lie behind unbridled capitalism, the most important of which is unrestrained individual self-fulfilment. In pursuit of this God (idolatry is anything but dead) the advertising industry attempts to increase desire infinitely for the sake of profit. Restraints have to be fought for: the introduction of full or partial bans on advertising alcohol in France, Russia and parts of Scandinavia is a testimony to what can be done. Battles like this expose a core value: the common good. Important as individual needs are, they need to be balanced by the good of society as a whole. In this context the individual is seen not as a commodity to be manipulated but as an unassailable value in him or herself – in Christian terms, a son or daughter of God – and also part of that wider family of God that includes everyone.

The key contribution that Christianity can make to these problems is precisely the value it places on individuals as part of a wider community. So the rights of each person or group, while unique and inalienable, have to be evaluated in the wider context of the common good. The framers of the Universal Declaration on Human Rights were correct to focus on the individual in the light of the slaughters of the twentieth century. That focus, however, needs to be balanced – without detracting from respect for the individual – by recognising that God calls us not only as individuals but also as a people. The story of Christianity, coming from its Jewish roots, can be seen as a slow coming to the realisation that the chosen people, while still being Our Lord's own people, the Jewish people, includes also all others in the world.

Local concerns

At a local level our focus is necessarily more limited: peace-making in Northern Ireland and social issues. We face a dilemma in this section: we need to address issues that are specific to our situation, and to do so in some detail. At the same time the issues which we find urgent will differ from those which people in other countries and in other contexts find urgent. Our issues will not be your issues. Yet, it is worth asking: in the light of what we have written about the life and values of Christ, what are the implications for you, in the way you approach social and political issues in your own context? How do you apply the values of Christ – trying to overcome enmity, respecting those with whom you disagree, being open to diversity, having compassion for those who have suffered – to your actual concrete situation? We find ourselves challenged by this question, and we suspect that the same will be true for you.

Chapter 10: The Past

All our ministry has been carried on in the context of the latest phase of violent conflict in Northern Ireland. Thankfully, major violence has declined since the Good Friday Agreement of 1998, but our society remains deeply divided. How should we as Christians respond to this? In particular how should we respond to major disagreements about how we deal with our past?

This is a question many want to avoid, and for understandable reasons. It is not relevant to their context. That is true of many in Northern Ireland, as well as in other countries.

The problem is that nearly all societies coming out of conflict struggle with dealing with the past. If one side wins then it gets to write the history of that conflict. But in Northern Ireland no side won. So we are left with disagreement about both the present and the past. And that disagreement is one factor that keeps us divided and also demands a large amount of resources through police work, courts, and the impact of trauma on the health costs of those who were bereaved and wounded, both psychologically and physically. So it is important that we address it.

Violence
Opposing IRA and Loyalist violence was central to our work as Christian ministers, as was challenging abuses by the security forces.

Republicans

Republican ideology in the past claimed that the British government illegally invaded and occupied Ireland, that sectarianism in Northern Ireland was a symptom of British imperialism and that the solution to sectarian violence was the withdrawal of the British government, something that could, in their view, only be achieved by force. Therefore, in each generation men and women took up arms to fight for Irish freedom. The 'war' is now over, however. The way to achieve Republican aims now, according to Sinn Fein, is through politics and persuasion, and in this 'post-war' context violence is wrong. Nonetheless, the violence of the past was justified. Those who took part in it and were killed by British forces are to be seen as 'martyrs', and deserve to be celebrated as such.

The above view is incorrect: the violence was morally wrong. It was also politically self-destructive. Nationalists faced a choice in 1968. The suffered real injustices. One way to respond was through violence. That option had been used in the 1916 Rising by a small minority and it was eventually enshrined as the basis of the freedom of the southern state. In itself this was tragic. Throughout the nineteenth century violence had been far less important and effective as a means of winning concessions for Catholics than constitutional means: Daniel O'Connell's monster meetings brought emancipation in 1832; Charles Stewart Parnell and Michael Davitt (a Fenian, but one who for the most part used non-violent means) between them, and with the help of British Prime Minister William Gladstone, put home rule at the very top of the British government's agenda. John Redmond won British government agreement for the implementation of home rule at the end of the First World War. Nonetheless when the 1921 Treaty led to a large degree of independence for the Republic, the myth of violent revolution was chosen as the basis of the new southern state, and tens of thousands of Irishmen who had fought with British forces in the fields of Flanders were written out of history.

Armed resistance was not the only option open to Catholics in 1968, but because of the glorification of 1916 it was highly tempting. Another approach was that adopted by the majority of Nationalists: constitutionalism, heavily influenced by the Civil Rights movement in the US. It was a major tragedy that the spirituality of peace, with its focus of loving the enemy, while it was ingrained in the majority, did not penetrate so deeply enough into the Nationalist community to rule out the option of violence altogether.

The important point to note, however, is that Nationalists had a choice between constitutional politics, with all its frustrations and limits, and violence. It is easy for both of us to understand why Republicans used violence, because that is always a tempting option. But it is also important to assess the justification for doing so, and when we do this it seems to us that it was the wrong choice, both morally and politically. The same is true for Loyalists.

Loyalists

Loyalists argue that they were reacting to Republican attacks. There will never be agreement about who threw the first stone, but even if Republicans did, there was not a shred of justification for the terrible killings carried out by Loyalists. They were just as morally wrong as any other murder.

However, Loyalists are scapegoats within the Protestant community. The dominant narrative is that the British government engaged in a police action against terrorists and criminals. There was no war. The government operated within the norms of a Western democratic state. From this point of view Loyalists were terrorists and criminals.

It is quite a different narrative from the Republican one, which sees the IRA fighting for Irish freedom against a colonial power.

All these narratives are false. The British government did not follow the norms of a Western democratic state. While many thousands who served in the security forces did so honourably, there are too many documented cases – for example, the cover-up of Bloody Sunday, and the abuses exposed by the O'Loan enquiry – to pretend that the government did not often meet terrorism with terrorism. Making this point does not minimise or excuse what Loyalist or Republican paramilitaries did. It does, however, mean that others cannot be self-righteous.

From the 1920–70s many in the Unionist middle and upper classes provided direct leadership for paramilitaries. This was not the case from 1970 on. Many did, however, provide encouragement, and so they have no basis for self-righteousness. Those others, even, who neither engaged in the violence nor encouraged it, cannot be self-righteous either: all of us have our own sins to live with.

Loyalists now face difficult choices: they backed the British state, and it now suits the British state to disown them. It was always part of the Loyalist approach that they would mobilise to defend their country in a time of crisis, and when this crisis was over they would withdraw. Yet, this meant that the Democratic Unionist Party (DUP) moved into the political space they left, and many Loyalists feel the DUP are not involved in working class areas. This means that working class Loyalists need their own political vehicle.

They have this to an extent in the Progressive Unionist Party (PUP). Yet, to make political progress they need to deal with a number of issues. One such issue is the use of arms: working class areas are plagued by drugs, the police response to this, rightly or wrongly, is often seen as inadequate, and this means the temptation to use violence is very high. Insofar as Loyalists do this they cannot claim to be good British citizens, because part of being a British citizen is recognising that only the state forces have a legal right to bear arms.

A second, and related issue is that some Loyalist areas are known to be involved in drug dealing. Insofar as this is the case all Loyalists will be tarred with the same brush. They need therefore to deal with the following dilemma: cutting off these areas will help to clean up the image of Loyalism, but at the same time it will reduce the influence progressive Loyalists have over the drug barons.

It has certainly been the case that Republicans have got a much easier ride on many of these issues. Despite being linked with violent crime and other criminalities, including diesel laundering, they have not, as yet, faced heavy political consequences. There is nothing Loyalists can do about this. If they want to make political progress themselves, then they will have to be seen to clean up their act.

Security forces

For their part, there were many instances of collusion between the security forces and paramilitaries. This was not only with Loyalists: British penetration of the IRA was at a very high level, including a mole code-named 'stakeknife', who played a leading role within the IRA, killing people that the organisation deemed to be informers. At the time of writing cases are pending which may well overturn convictions of paramilitaries, and this is likely to lead to successful claims against the state for wrongful convictions. This is one of many examples of the cost to the state of dealing with the past, a cost borne not only in the suffering of victims, but also by the taxpayers. Investigating historical cases is also a major drain on police resources.

Some politicians were also guilty because they directed or allowed the security forces to do wrong. There was no moral or legal justification for members of the security forces to kill people, except in self-defence or when necessary to protect the lives of others. 'Minimum force' is a principle that should govern police and military in all democratic societies.

We in Ireland know only too well the consequences of giving in to the temptation to violence. The same is true of conflict worldwide: in almost every situation those who choose violence end up killing more of their own than others. They divide their own community, and they abuse the very values they proclaim. IRA 'trials' of so-called informers breached almost every standard of human rights and these were often carried out at the same time that the IRA was protesting against British judicial abuses. Collusion with paramilitaries by the security forces contradicted the very values that the British government claimed to be upholding in Northern Ireland.

Disputed legitimacy of the state

Unionists continue to stress that Northern Ireland is part of the United Kingdom – which is correct. Many argue that it should be governed by straight majority rule, as is the case with other democracies, although this is now never going to happen: Nationalists are too strong to allow it. For their part Nationalists are divided. The Social Democratic Labour Party (SDLP) accepted the principle of consent in the 1998 Agreement which meant that there could be no change in the constitutional status of Northern Ireland without the consent of the majority of people in both Northern Ireland and the Republic. Sinn Fein accepted the Agreement, but acted as if Northern Ireland did not exist. Both they and the SDLP almost always avoid the term 'Northern Ireland' and instead refer to it as 'The North' or 'The Six Counties'. When they entered government, Sinn Fein Ministers used 'Beal Feirste', the Irish for Belfast, as the address of their offices, with no designation of the country. They also frequently spoke as if the move to a united Ireland was inevitable.

Unionists and Republicans reject each other's moral evaluation of the conflict. For most Unionists it was a struggle against terrorists in which many brave soldiers and police officers lost their lives. For

Republicans it was a war for Irish freedom in which their volunteers were murdered by state forces The logic of this latter position would subject all combatants to the legislation that governs war crimes, and if this were so Republicans would face punishment for their own atrocities, as would the British state.

Commemorations

Commemorations of deceased paramilitaries are a real problem for those who see all paramilitary activity as wrong. If we are to move forward in peace, groups need first to take account of the impact of our commemorations on opposing groups. Secondly, opposing groups need to accept that it is unlikely that we will ever agree about the past, and that therefore we have to give space to others to remember their dead in a way that they see fit.

Putting those two principles together will never be easy. It would help if paramilitary commemorations were not held in or near areas where a significant proportion of opposing groups live or where a significant minority might object, but are afraid to do so. The principle is fairly obvious: Northern Ireland is a divided society. We need to live together. We therefore have to avoid actions that are seen by others as gratuitously offensive, unless it is a case of a minority group which is unable to express its opinion or identity in any other way. Even this last condition has to be limited by the public good.

It would help if speeches at these events emphasised that now that the violence has ended former enemies are citizens together, and as such have duties and responsibilities to each other.

Paramilitaries will argue that they have as much right to commemorate their dead volunteers as the British state has to remember its war dead on Remembrance Sunday. We disagree, despite all the wrongs committed by the British army. Paramilitaries, however, are never going to agree with us about this. Given this reality how can we live together in the future?

UK-wide remembrance ceremonies are going to continue, but they are about *all* British war dead, not only those killed in the Troubles. As with similar ceremonies in other states, a certain ambivalence is appropriate about these events. On the one hand they are legitimate commemorations of those who gave their lives on behalf of the state. On the other hand they can easily enforce the militarism of the British state. Few people comment on this: yet the number of occasions on which military are used on state occasions, such as royal events, is striking. These events subliminally reinforce the legitimacy of war, and surely encourage young men to join the armed forces. This is an important issue given the number of wars in which the UK has been involved. The British state is in a weak position to lecture Republicans about violence. Obviously in Northern Ireland there is the added dimension of divisions in attitudes towards the state. Churches should dialogue with each other about these issues.

In many Anglican churches there are a range of flags and banners. Some of these belong to youth organisations such as the scouts and guides; others are historical items, such as regimental standards and Ulster Volunteer Force (UVF) flags. These can cause huge problems, as events in Newry (when the rector unilaterally removed and burnt a British Legion flag in October 2015) show all too clearly. The rector's intention was to remove a symbol that might cause problems for some members of the Nationalist community, but in so doing, and doing so without consultation and in such a dramatic fashion, he alienated many within his own community.

For many these flags have huge sentimental importance, for others they are a deeply unhelpful statement of tribal loyalty in a divided society. For both of us this is a very real issue which needs to be tackled sensitively and through dialogue

It is not for the clergy to take unilateral action. If action is to be taken, it needs to be agreed. That takes time and patience. In informal discussions Tim has often found that many within the Church of Ireland community at least are aware of the difficulties that such flags and emblems pose – yet both he and they feel that to push the issue would be unnecessarily divisive. Similarly, many from the 'other side' also recognise the dilemma. It is sometimes a case of letting sleeping dogs lie; it is a case of treating the 'offending' flags and emblems as historical documents rather than currently provocative symbols.

Perhaps the best way to deal with divisive issues such as flags, emblems and commemorations is through local dialogue and discernment. Compromise can often be reached, for instance by moving the flags to a less prominent position, or into a church hall rather than the church itself. Above all, it needs to be recognised that Church membership – our being 'in Christ' – should transcend (although not deny) our sense of physical and tribal identity. That realisation is not achieved overnight.

Parades

Parades are a reflection of the insecurity of Protestants and the communal resentment of Nationalists. In a divided society symbols matter.

In fact great progress has been made over the years so that now only a small number of the 3000 plus parades that take place annually are contentious. This progress has been made because people in different communities, business people, churches and the security forces decided to enter dialogue and to make the necessary compromises. Nonetheless, the cost of policing these is considerable, and often leads to injuries to police officers and others.

Parades and protests against them matter to a significant minority – over 30,000 are members of Loyalist bands. To the rest of the population, however, they are for the most part minor nuisances.

In the USA the constitution guarantees the right to freedom of speech.

On that basis courts are likely to give any group the legal right to march where they want, irrespective of how insulting others may find this. In practice, however, police, for operational reasons, may decide to block or re-route a parade (this was the outcome of the parade in Chicago when a neo-Nazi group wanted to march through a Jewish area).

There are pros and cons to this approach. The UK does not have a written constitution. Further, judges for many years have avoided as much as possible having a direct say over the legality of parades (they normally get involved through judicial reviews). Instead a government appointed quango, the Parades Commission, is tasked with decisions. Inevitably it is criticised and Unionists, especially, call for its removal.

There are two alternatives to a parades commission: having judges make the decisions, or having the police make them. The latter was the practise for many years and it was a bad one: police are asked to implement, not to make, the law. Unless one wants judges to take over all decisions in this area, which would take up an enormous amount of their time, and apparently meet great resistance from judges, the only alternative is some form of a parades commission.

Some principles should govern decisions:

◆ Minority rights should be privileged. Democracy has some basic principles: government must rule in a way that respects minorities. The application of principles is always a matter of judgement; so it seems fair to say in general that Loyal Orders should have greater rights in Londonderry, for example, (because there they are a minority) and less rights in Portadown (because there they are a majority).

◆ In the absence of communal agreement rights talk is often used simply as another weapon in conflict. While rights have always to be respected, an ordered and fair society can only develop if individual and group rights are part of a wider context, one in which each group recognises that the basis of its own rights requires respect for the rights of others.

- ◆ While the expression of identity or opinion is a right and should be protected it needs to be balanced against the rights of the wider public not to have their lives disrupted. So it is appropriate that a group be allowed to parade in a town centre, thus disrupting traffic, once a year, or perhaps twice or even three times. It is not at all clear that they should be allowed to do so forty times, as occasionally happens. Groups without finance should be supported freely by the state when this is necessary to allow them to express their opinion. Yet, moderation demands that this happens only on a limited number of occasions. In line with this policy of moderation, security costs for parades, when a group has had the opportunity to express themselves on several occasions already, should be met by the parade organisers.
- ◆ There should be a fast court system for breaches of public order in regard to parades whether by those taking part or by protesters. Decisions about future parades and protests should also take account of breaches of public order. That might mean that a parade or a protest is banned the following year.

There are real signs of hope Republicans have made significant and difficult gestures in the peace process: on several occasions they have taken part in Remembrance Day ceremonies, thereby honouring their enemies. Most dramatically, Martin McGuinness attended the state banquet during the 2014 visit by President Higgins to Britain and at that banquet stood to toast the Queen. No one should underestimate the difficulty involved in doing this for anyone from a Republican background.

The British state, too, has made dramatic gestures, perhaps most notably the gesture by Queen Elizabeth when she bowed her head at the Garden of Remembrance in Dublin in 2011. Such efforts at dialogue and understanding need to continue and to be increased.

Chapter 11: Responding To Those Who Suffered

'Innocent victims'

The division about the past has led to disputes about the treatment of those who suffered in the conflict. On one view, held by many Protestants, 'innocent victims' were killed by Republicans – who themselves were seen as terrorists and murderers. Those who hold this position are deeply offended that Sinn Fein is now in government. They argue that Republicans had no moral basis for their campaign of violence. Therefore every Republican killing was murder. Sinn Fein should, therefore, be rejected by the rest of society, not elected into political office. They find it particularly offensive that Republicans glorify their dead 'martyrs'. On the view of the 'innocent victims' this is simply glorifying terrorism.

We have used inverted commas in the above paragraph quite deliberately around the terms 'innocent victims' and 'martyrs'. Both are terms which make moral assumptions that for the most part we reject.

However, there is a partial truth in the 'innocent victim' designation, in that the suffering of many was brought about by their being in the wrong place at the wrong time. They were not fighters who took the calculated risk that their involvement might, amongst other things, result in their own injury or death. They were bystanders:

Here are the graves of all the poor and innocent
Who died in civil tumult and in war.
Here is the tombstone of a child
Who found a bomb;
And here the grave of the young mother
Who was caught in crossfire
And never saw her son mature.
Tragic ends for chosen people,
Holy victims of a wicked war;
They were sacrificed for nothing,
Yet theirs is peace for evermore.
(early poem by Tim Kinahan, from 1975).

So of those who suffered the loss of life, or physical or psychological trauma, who was innocent? Children were. So were many adults who were innocent of any wrong doing relating to the Troubles. Some of these did not belong to the security forces or to any paramilitary group. Other innocents were in the security forces: they joined from high ideals and they paid the ultimate price.

Paramilitaries who resorted to violence were morally wrong. In this sense those who reject a moral equivalence between the security forces and paramilitaries are correct: the security forces were in principle acting on behalf of a government that, however badly its forces acted at times, enjoyed a degree of legitimacy. To reject this is to argue that the British government had no right to run any sort of police force, or to control an army which could be used to defuse bombs, or to raise taxes, to run schools or hospitals, to provide roads and to do all those things that governments do in modern society.

While we reject the moral equation of security forces and paramilitaries, and while we also reject completely the morality of paramilitary violence, we do not accept the blanket assumption of innocence applied by some to the security forces. This is not simply a case of a few bad apples. Eighteen members of the UDR (a full regiment of the British army) were convicted of murder, and eleven of manslaughter. Given that the courts often accepted the defence argument that soldiers thought the person they killed had a gun, this is a high figure.

Many other members of the security forces acted with incredible bravery. Over 2000 were killed, the vast majority by Republicans.

Those like ourselves who were neither members of the security forces nor of paramilitary groups may think that we are morally superior. We are not, because we are sinners in other areas: 'let him or her without sin cast the first stone' (*Jn. 8*). We may also have added to the sectarianism which in turn contributed to violence, or we may have failed to do things we could have done to reduce such sectarianism.

Victims or survivors?

Individuals face their own tough journey to deal with the pain of losing loved ones. Others can support and help.

Only people going through the experience, however, know what this is like for them. Only they can, in the end, find ways to move to a place where they are less dominated by the loss. Several things make it more difficult for people to do this.

One is the sheer length of investigations, trials and inquests. It is incredible that twenty years and more after a killing some inquests have not been held. In some cases the reason is the refusal of government to give access to papers. Sometimes this is to protect agents or individuals who have information. In other cases it is to protect the government from embarrassment. Surely some kind of privy council system could be designed to protect vulnerable individuals. It is seriously wrong that relatives are kept hanging in suspense because of the failure to complete legal proceedings.

A second difficulty is that there are financial benefits to people in Northern Ireland who identify themselves as victims. An on-going debate focuses on how much payments to them should be.

A third difficulty is that the failure to get any widespread consensus about how to deal with the past means discussion of it, with media attention, continues. If an issue is always in the news it is harder for those who have suffered to think of other things. This point is well known by those who work with people who have suffered sexual abuse.

A fourth is that many paramilitaries are now in public life in Northern Ireland. Further, because we live in a small place, those who killed and those who lost loved ones often live in the same towns or neighbourhoods. That means that people meet the killers in the local supermarket and post office. Dealing with the past is often personal.

A fifth difficulty is that many are both victims and oppressors: paramilitaries who have killed people may themselves have been subjected to injustice.

A sixth is that people can take on the identity of victimhood as if that is the only identity they have. Yet, all of us have multiple identities: as fathers, mothers, aunts, uncles, community workers, artists, husbands, wives, partners and lovers. An over-emphasis on any one identity can only distort the reality. An 'innocent victim' is very far from all any victim is: it may well be the most painful part of who they are right now, but to say that it is fundamental to who they are is to take an incomplete view. Victimhood is a passive state, something suffered rather than lived: to remain a victim is to continue to suffer. The alternative is to follow the long hard road to let go of victimhood and find liberation, or – to use theological language – salvation. What is needed is a sympathetic realism; to live fully we must leave victimhood behind for the sake of both individual liberation and community integrity. This is easy to say but very hard to achieve.

Ways to respond to the past

Many countries, such as South Africa, have used some sort of truth commission to deal with the past. This is unlikely to work in Northern Ireland: in South Africa one side won, the African National Congress (ANC) became the government. In Northern Ireland neither side won outright. Generally, the pressure needs to be very high for organisations and groups to admit wrong doing voluntarily. Given that neither side lost, or at least that neither is generally perceived to have lost, we cannot see how sufficient pressure can be brought on the British government, Republicans or Loyalists for a truth commission to work.

In the absence of a truth commission we will continue to be drip fed with stories of wrong doing. One of many examples is a spate of stories that appeared in early 2016. Some of these emerged because Lord Justice Weir was appointed to review fifty-six inquests that had never been held for people killed decades before. One concerned Sean Brown who was abducted and murdered by Loyalists in 1997. The judge heavily criticised the failure of the police to produce the necessary paperwork. The police responded that there was a vast number of papers and each had to be reviewed for reasons of state security and the protection of informers. 'Redactions should not vary depending on the state of digestion of the person carrying it out on any one day', the judge said and gave a two week deadline. In fact both the judge and the police have a point: it is outrageous that these inquests have never been held, but it is also true that dealing with the past in cases such as this takes up major police resources.

A second story was on the inquest of a Catholic Royal Ulster Constabulary (RUC) officer, Joseph Campbell, shot dead in February 1977. John Larkin, QC, ordered a new inquest after fresh evidence was presented, including a Police Ombudsman's report in 2014 which claimed that the RUC chief Constable 'quite probably' knew about the threat to Constable Campbell, but failed to act.

A third story in the *Irish News* reported that the head of the IRA in the Ardoyne had been a British agent, code named 'AA', that he had prior knowledge of the Shankill bomb on 23 October 1993 and that he had informed his handlers, who allowed the bombing to go ahead. Further, the report claimed that the IRA had known about the agent from shortly after the 2002 breaking in to Castlereagh barracks, when they seized a considerable amount of Special Branch papers.

A second question raised by this and other stories is: what rules governed the use of informers? Who approved these rules? What politicians in government knew about them? Was political approval sought or given for any operations?

Perhaps the majority of stories that emerge will be of state wrong doing because they are likely to come from legal processes brought by relatives of the dead. This means that there is an imbalance in the process: Republican or Loyalist wrong doing – wrong even by their own standards – may be exposed less often.

This re-enforces what happens already: Republicans, many times with merit, complain about British government wrongdoing. They do so, however, self-righteously, as if they themselves were paragons of virtue. Nary a word said about the torture and killing of suspected informers. From what moral basis do they complain about wrongdoing by the state? Others, who believe that it was immoral to torture and kill people, have a right and a duty to challenge the state for the terrible wrongs done by state employees, but anyone who accepts such brutality themselves cannot do so with credibility

If a truth commission is not a likely way forward what other options are there? One is the launch of several inquiries. This immediately raises the spectre of the inquiry into Bloody Sunday, which cost hundreds of millions of pounds. Further, inquiries are inevitably into wrongdoing by the state. So how can they help the need for a balanced approach to the past?

There are examples of effective inquiries which cost vastly less than Bloody Sunday, such as that conducted by Nuala O'Loan into collusion in north Belfast. There may be merit in having a small number of further similar inquiries. These would show the extent of collusion between the state and paramilitaries, but they would also do something more: collusion was not only between the state and Loyalists but also between the security forces and the IRA. We know this because of the number of individuals within the IRA who have been outed as state agents. Inquiries are likely to expose more of this. So while such inquiries will certainly embarrass the state they are also likely to embarrass both Republicans and Loyalists. The outcome might then encourage a view that sees the past not as a glorious struggle for Irish freedom, or for democracy against terrorism, but rather as a bloody and corrupt disaster. Security force members who served with high ideals to defend their country will find themselves deeply troubled by such findings. The findings will not, however, undermine the honourable service that so many of these men and women gave. It will simply highlight the tendency that exists in all organisations, especially in conflict, to move toward corruption. All organisations benefit from facing that reality, owning up to what individuals have done, and taking responsibility for morally wrong decisions made by senior management.

British security forces, Republicans and Loyalists all did wrong. Each needs to admit this, not in some generic sense, but in a very specific way that accounts for each individual killing. To take responsibility for each killing, to apologise for it, to commit themselves to work for peace and to remember their own members who died in a way that recognises and takes account of the killings they did or that they supported, that surely would be a contribution to the future. Such acknowledgement could be done in a collective way so that individuals did not become legally liable. To those who say they might be open to something like this only if others did it there is a simple answer: each group needs to make such an acknowledgement because that is the right thing to do, given our past.

A hopeful outcome of all this might be that we would cease glorifying the past, that Republicans would give up trying to put the government in the dock, and that the state might apologise for the wrong it did. All sides need to refrain from self-righteously criticizing each other. The impact of such apologies should not be underestimated: British Prime Minister David Cameron's apology for Bloody Sunday in 2010 made a deep impact.

All this would be in harmony with Christian values. But is such a process not inherently lacking in balance, since the IRA would not apologise for the killings that it carried out but which it regarded as legitimate? Yes, it would lack balance. We can only look for balance, however, if we think that the government and the IRA are equal. What made collusion wrong in the case of the government was that it was against all the norms of Western civilised governments, norms which the British government claimed to be defending. If the government admits to more collusion, or if this is proved, then it is entirely appropriate to apologise for it. What made IRA killings wrong is that the so-called war was never legitimate: while Catholics certainly suffered oppression and discrimination, killing in response to this was never justified. Yet, this is a view that Republicans reject. Hence, the embarrassment for Republicans from enquiries will come, not because it will expose their killings, but because it will expose the degree to which they were penetrated by British security. That may temper their desire to glorify the past.

No approach can bring justice

People wronged in the Troubles want justice and are entitled to it. They are unlikely to get it because the passage of time has made evidence, if it can ever be unearthed, less reliable, and because there is no agreement about a process to deal with the past.

The International Court of Human Rights is a relatively new effort to ensure that those who commit atrocities during conflicts do not get away with it. It has not been a great success. To date only a few have been convicted. Africans understandably criticise it because almost all those tried have been from their continent. It is especially wrong that the US Government will not subject its own forces to the authority of the court. That preaches a simple message: might is right. That is the opposite of the message that the Court is trying to proclaim, and the opposite of the values of Christ.

In Northern Ireland neither the British nor the Irish governments have much appetite for justice because if paramilitaries are prosecuted they will threaten more violence. This often is what is meant by phrases such as 'endangering the peace process'.

In the absence of agreement between the DUP and Sinn Fein, many want the two governments to impose some form of amnesty for troubles-related killings up to the date of the 1998 Agreement. This may well be the best way forward, but human rights legislation may throw up legal blocks to it. If the governments choose not to impose an amnesty or are prevented from doing so, then we will be left with the status quo: drip-feed disclosures of wrong doing by security force members with few being brought to court, and some focus on paramilitary crime.

Huge numbers were hurt in the past. Many are now no longer dominated by this hurt. Others continue with raw pain. Thousands who did not suffer the loss of loved ones are tired of the never-ending deadlock. All this will continue unless the two main political parties agree or at least tolerate a settlement imposed by the two governments. That shows the deep need we have for genuine and courageous political leadership in Northern Ireland.

Peace and justice

Our dreams include peace and justice, but it turns out, in common with most conflicts in the world, that there is a tension between these. 'Justice' is a contested term in divided societies. It is not enough to proclaim that one is working for justice unless one also shows how a demand is just for other communities as well as one's own.

During the Troubles Churches were often accused of being chaplains to their own people. While true to an extent, it is also the case that a great number of those who worked for peace did so out of Christian conviction.

Jesus and outcasts

Our enemies are outcasts: they are not seen as part of our community. In the language of Northern Ireland they are 'not one of ours'.

We have already seen in chapter 8 that in his encounter with the Caananite woman Jesus had to learn how to deal with those different from himself in cultural identity. We have seen too how he reached out to sinners and outcasts. A startling example of this was his meeting with the tax collector, Zacchaeus (*Lk.19*). Zacchaeus was a small man, and he wanted to see Jesus who had just come into Jericho. So he ran ahead of the crowd and climbed up a tree. Jesus stopped underneath him and told him that he was going to stay with him that night.

Why choose Zacchaeus? He was not only a tax collector but a leading one. That meant he was a major oppressor of the people. Colluding with the Romans, the tax collectors exacted as much as they could from a population that was barely subsisting. And in doing so they colluded in blasphemy: by their very presence in Palestine the Romans polluted the holy places. For the onlookers the decision of Jesus to stay with Zacchaeus was hugely offensive.

Nor was Zacchaeus' repentance total: he may have been willing to give half of what he owed to the poor when Jesus offered to stay with him. But what about the other half? Where had that come from? Yet Jesus chose him: 'Today salvation has come to this house, because this man, too, is a son of Abraham. For the Son of Man came to seek and to save the lost' (*Lk.19:9*).

Christians therefore have a duty to reach out to their enemies, even to engage with people who may currently be oppressing their communities. This reaching out is not about accepting or minimising wrong: rather it is about trying to build relationships of truth through which oppressors may change.

Both of us have had different experiences within our respective communities.

For sixteen years Brian lived in Iona, a Jesuit community in what was then a marginalised housing estate in Portadown. He worked with local residents on community and economic projects. That was a clear response to a need for justice. It was striking how much money was raised in the local Catholic community for the Third World, but how little focus there was on the terrible unemployment locally. Gradually, through the valiant efforts of a small group of local residents some projects succeeded: a small youth club was set up – it was known as the 'Cabin Club' because it started in a small hut, like so many other similar projects in Northern Ireland. Eventually, a community centre was built, and a large leasing company owned by the local trust was set up with the active support of a local carpet factory.

The aim of Brian and the other Jesuits in the community was to work for justice *and* peace. One could not exist without the other. But 'justice' meant justice for Unionists as well as Nationalists. That aim was ambitious. On the one hand it meant supporting locals who opposed Protestant Orange marches going through their area, because they saw those marches as an exercise in domination. Their reaction was understandable. There were about forty-five parades in the town centre every summer. While these parades were accepted by Nationalists, they did not accept the two parades that went through the Nationalist area on the twelfth and again on the thirteenth of July, nor did they accept the Church parade on the Sunday before the twelfth of July.

This was not a new problem. Over the centuries there has often been conflict at these parades.

An Orange myth grew up that the Jesuits were moved into Portadown in order to block the parades. It was only in recent years after several meetings with Brian that a senior Orangeman accepted that this was not true. In fact the second aspect of our work – peace as well as justice – meant that we worked to understand Unionists ourselves and to help local people to do so as well. Our own understanding was helped by the Faith and Politics Group, and also by the varied people from other denominations and viewpoints that we met through our ecumenical and community contacts.

Justice also meant challenging Nationalists. A small group of Nationalists formed the 'Drumcree Faith and Justice Group' which insisted that the only way to oppose Orange marches through the area was to do so non-violently. What Orangemen did not see – because of segregation – was that this was as much a challenge to the IRA as it was to the Orangemen. Indeed this small group showed great courage in canvassing local residents to oppose IRA killings and so-called 'punishment shootings'. This group also produced a small pamphlet *The Story of A Journey* [11] in which, having reflected on different Christian stories, they asked themselves how they were called to respond to their enemies in the conflict.

At the same time as Brian was working in Portadown, Tim was rector of a parish on the 'peace-line' in West Belfast. His first year there (having just returned from his three year stint in Papua New Guinea) was spent listening to and getting to know the community –

church goers, agnostics, atheists, paramilitaries, community workers and everybody in between.

It was then that Tim set up a parish project designed to meet some of the needs identified within the community: alienation, poverty, paramilitarism, sectarianism, ill-health and so on. Funding was arranged, staff hired and projects initiated. Ecumenical contacts were ratcheted up, benefit take-up campaigns were supported, paramilitary racketeering exposed and publicly challenged (in cooperation with Roman Catholic colleagues across the peace-line), a Health Fair held, a playgroup initiated (run by the Save the Children Fund), prisoners' families supported ... and so on: justice, social action, time spent with those on the margins of society.

With the wisdom of hindsight this project was less successful that it might have been, and for two main reasons:

1. It was the rector's baby, his answer to real local questions. Had Tim spent more time listening, he might have been able to initiate more broadly-based programmes with deeper local support that would survive after he had left. It was one man's baby, insufficiently rooted.

2. Although the local Church community was, at one level, proud to be associated with what was being done in their name, they did not buy into it as *their* project. Some amongst them felt that they were being neglected while others, who had never darkened the door of a church, were taking up all the Church's time and resources.

But at least something was attempted. Issues were grappled with and a real attempt made to work out the implication of the gospel at the local level. It is a project still remembered with gratitude.

Chapter 12: Making Peace

Much of the peace work in Northern Ireland goes under the umbrella of 'reconciliation'. As a political theme it is particularly attractive to Christians, so much so that some would see it as an umbrella concept to describe everything Churches are called to be and to do. Christ came to reconcile the world to the blessed Trinity, to bring groups into relationship with each other, to break down enmity (*Eph. 2:10*) and to persuade people to repent. For Christ the cross was initially a failure because he wanted people to accept his message of love, truth, honesty, solidarity and compassion. Yet, the cross turned out to be the means of his victory, because in the face of persecution, hatred, division and murder he responded with total love, with a call to repentance and with an offer of complete forgiveness: he restored, indeed created anew, a full relationship with God.

The wars and other violent conflicts of our time, the deaths imposed and the suffering endured, the expulsion of refugees and the hunger of millions, all these bring tears to the heart of Christ. The Christian, then, is surely called to work for reconciliation.

Dialogue

We should not, however, move directly from an idea found in Scripture or theology to the realm of politics. Not all contexts are the same.

Brian has been involved in a dialogue process for nearly thirty years. It has been a truly useful instrument, and has helped to break down much enmity. With others he was a founder member of a project called 'Community Dialogue' which invited people in more deprived areas to meet their enemies. Often efforts like this bring together people who are concerned about conflict, but have no real differences among themselves. Community Dialogue instead focused on those who had most difficulties with other groups, who were passionate in their opposition and who often were part of groups that either had killed relatives of other participants, or had lost relatives themselves in the conflict.

The process focused on a basic question: 'What is it that really matters most to you?' In the course of the dialogues, which were often residential and lasted for several days, people gradually moved from headline issues to more basic matters like their children, stories of their loved ones who had been killed in the Troubles – often by organisations to which other participants belonged – and health care. This led to understanding. People began to see why others acted as they did. There was rarely agreement, but the sharing of stories opened up common experiences. That transformed relationships.

Those who participated in Community Dialogue also worked at understanding the dynamics of conflict. We were greatly helped in this by social psychologists at Stanford University, especially Byron Bland and Lee Ross, and a joint project with them ran for three years. Part of this involved bringing divided groups to Stanford to take part in difficult conversations. One great advantage was that participants learnt about conflicts in other areas, and were able to identify similar dynamics in some of them.

What has been the outcome of this and similar initiatives? Well, ask people in interface areas where there has been such dialogue: yes, there are still many difficulties, but mobile phone communication has reduced rumours and helped manage immediate conflict. Many groups have decided to work seriously together (as distinct from pretending to do so for funding applications that emphasise 'reconciliation'), and have developed serious economic, social and cultural initiatives based on mutual respect.

The Faith and Politics Group

As mentioned, both authors were founding members of The Inter-Church Group on Faith and Politics. The group was started following a talk by Brian at the Greenhills Ecumenical Conference in 1983. A group of clergy and laity from both Northern Ireland and the Republic came together to discern how to respond to the Troubles in the light of the Christian message. We did so because it was clear that our Churches were unable to do this at an official level. It took a long time to build trust among ourselves, but when we did it gradually became important to us to make as much space for the other person as for ourselves. The group was in some ways a clearing house where we could process our thinking and feelings about what was going on inside our own section of the community, and learn what was happening in other sections. That led to understanding: the bad things other communities did to our own became comprehensible. So did their fears. Understanding these fears enabled us to explain them to our own people. This understanding within the group was probably more important than the pamphlets we produced. So also was the fact that we were standing together as Christians coming from divided communities.

Many in the group were involved in quiet conversations with politicians, church people, paramilitaries and others, to try to increase understanding and communication, reduce violence and work slowly – tragically slowly – towards some kind of peace. In Brian's case this involved meetings with Billy Wright, a notorious loyalist killer in Portadown. These meetings were possible because Billy respected Church people. Billy was later killed by Republicans in the Maze prison. For Tim this involved much contact with paramilitaries and their families in his first parish. These relationships endured even when Tim, with Catholic colleagues, fronted a public campaign, including two TV programmes, against paramilitary racketeering in the building trade.

Dialogue is easier in some contexts than others. Brian was startled on one occasion at the end of a process in Liberia, when participants enthusiastically said that they wanted to apply the process to their own families. Why was he startled? Because dialogue within a family is different from dialogue among distinct tribes. In turn this is different from a process between countries that have been at war. There is a simple reason for this. Dialogue is easier, and may work better, to the extent that people are not in close interpersonal relations. So, soldiers who fought in a war fifty years ago will find it much easier to stand together in commemoration of it, than two brothers who were involved in a bitter conflict. In the war example, the conditions that led to it have almost certainly disappeared. (It is notable how quickly former enemies can work together in international relations after a conflict: West Germany and the USA were allies within a few years of the end of the Second World War). The soldiers do not live with each other. They only meet for commemorations – unless they have become personal friends. It is much easier to get on with people if you do not meet them often.

It is much more difficult to make peace with a family member. There is far more emotional investment in the family. The lives of family members have been intertwined in a way that can never happen to people who live in different countries. That is why it was easier to bring Republicans and Loyalists together in Northern Ireland and start a dialogue than would be the case with a family dispute, or even a dispute within a Church or similar group.

Here the example of the 'Continuing Indaba' process within the Anglican Communion has much to teach us. This was a process initiated in 2009 at the request of the primates of the Anglican Communion and which aimed, through intensive, theologically informed dialogue, to deepen relationships across the diversity of the Anglican Communion, especially between those who held 'irreconcilably' different opinions on subjects such as the ordination of women, human sexuality and views of Scripture, to name but a few. Inevitably the numbers involved were small, but the deep relationships made and the theological and spiritual insights gained were powerful. Those directly influenced by the process have returned to their home provinces and churches with a new openness; the trickle-down effect has been significant.

International peace making is very important but it may be easier to manage wars between countries than those within countries, and for the same reasons: in the latter people are living together and are likely to have a longer history of violence.

Reconciliation has at times been used wrongly to encourage people to stay in abusive relations. 'Love your enemies', 'Do good to those that hate you', 'Pray for those who persecute you', and other sayings of Jesus have at times been used for this end. Yet, no one is bound to stay in or to return to an abusive relationship. Indeed, while there may be occasions when a person might justifiably do this, for example, if he or she makes the – often questionable – judgement that children might suffer less by staying in a marriage, the bias must be against doing so. Jesus himself did not enter abusive relationships. He offers forgiveness. He reaches out to people. He died for us all. But he cannot enter into a mutual relationship with us unless, with his grace, we repent. So while our capacity to offer forgiveness is not dependent on repentance, being reconciled with our enemies is dependent on both forgiving and repenting.

That last statement, like so much in the complexity of peace making, needs to be qualified.

It is said that Jean Monnet, one of the founding fathers of the European Economic Community (EEC), was approached by a German who wanted to work with him: the German, not surprisingly, had been a member of the *Wehrmact* and had been one of the occupiers of France. Further, he was not prepared to apologise for it. Monnet, a Frenchman, told him that if he shared the values and aspirations that he, Monnet, and others had for Europe, then he was welcome to join them. So he joined. There was certainly not repentance in this exchange. There may have been forgiveness. Yet, there was also an outcome in which former enemies worked together to help create the EEC, which has, in the form of the modern day EU, become the greatest conflict management structure that the world has known, even given the level of bureaucracy and corruption in it. Anyone who doubts this has only to compare the history of Europe from 1870–1945 with that of 1945 to today. Northern Ireland, and to a lesser extent Spain, are the only areas in which major conflict took place within member states. The ferociously destructive wars between France, Germany and the UK are a thing of the past. That is an amazing outcome.

Clearly, Christians in Northern Ireland have a call to work for better social and political relationships. We have a long way to go. Apart from the issues mentioned above, segregation and sectarianism remain. Part of the 1998 Agreement involved setting up the Stormont Assembly on the sectarian rocks of Unionists and Nationalists (all Members of the Legislative Assembly – MLAs – have to designate themselves as 'Unionist', 'Nationalist' or 'Other'. A majority of Unionists and of Nationalists is required to approve contentious decisions). In our view this was a necessary part of the agreement, but we now need to find ways to move beyond this. Will we be stuck with the same rules in fifty years' time?

Segregation

Segregation is always an issue in divided societies. It is important to remember, however, that all societies are divided, if not by political, religious or ethnic conflict, then by income. Segregation makes stereotyping easy: if we only encounter a few members of another group, and all our encounters are negative – from our point of view – then we will likely see the whole group negatively.

Churches in every country reinforce this to the extent that they do not make efforts to include people from diverse backgrounds.

Between seventy per cent and ninety per cent of people in public housing in Northern Ireland live in areas that are least eighty per cent Catholic or Protestant. In 1998, at the time of the signing of the Good Friday Agreement, there were approximately eighteen barriers of various shapes and sizes dividing communities in Belfast. In 2013 there were ninety-nine.[12] By any measure, segregation is deep and long lasting. This is costly. A research project in 2006 estimated that spend on social housing alone was inflated by £24 million a year because of segregation. The Northern Ireland Life and Times Survey has shown consistently that a large majority of people would prefer to live in mixed-religion neighbourhoods: in 2010, eighty per cent of both Protestants and Catholics favoured this. There is a contradiction between this figure and the actual number of those who live in desegregated communities, and the Peace Monitoring Report suggests that this may be due either to respondents giving the answer that they suspect will please the questioner, or else because there are real, practical problems with greater integration.

The segregation that exists in Northern Ireland at one level is not surprising. The latest phase of the conflict ran from the mid-1960s to almost the present day. Over 3000 were killed. Over 40,000 went through the prisons. About the same number served in the security forces who were at the front line of the conflict. The violence did not end with victory for any side. Instead a 'sulky stalemate'[13] emerged.

There are no simple answers to segregation: all over the world people keep to those they see as 'their own'. When people are rich enough ethnic divisions may break down, but then the division between rich and poor is maintained.

The Church of Ireland set up its 'Hard Gospel' project in 2003, as part of an attempt to examine sectarianism. As its website says, the project 'represents a commitment by the Church of Ireland to examine not only the challenges of faith which arise for Christians in the "vertical" relationship in loving God but also the practical implications for the outworking of faith in "horizontal" relationships as expressed in Christ's command to "love your neighbour"'. It is a laudable commitment and an impressive project, but, as with all such projects, it is finding it very hard to make an impact on the ground. People lack time and enthusiasm. They view the issues as 'someone else's problem'. Despite this its approach is slowly trickling down to the parish level. Change is tentatively in the air. The slightly more narrowly focused 'Moving Beyond Sectarianism' project of the Irish School of Ecumenics, also impressive, has had a similarly limited if important impact.

The need to support and to challenge

Back in 1984, when Tim was appointed to the west Belfast parish of which he was rector for six years, he asked his congregation that all local clergy, including Roman Catholic neighbours, be invited to his institution. It soon became clear that, if he had insisted on this, several key people in the parish would have left. However, within a few years, with varying degrees of enthusiasm, all of those people had attended cross community events, prayer groups, Bible studies and so on, many of them at the ecumenical Cornerstone Community. Deep listening, gentle persuasion and real human contact proved more powerful than stubborn dogmatism.

It has always been clear to us that a key role of ministry is not only to support and comfort one's people but also to challenge them, especially in the area of peace making. In divided societies all Churches lack credibility if they do not engage in peace work. As we saw in Section 2, Jesus had to learn about diversity through being confronted by people different from himself, such as the Canaanite woman in Matthew 15, and the early Church had to go through a purifying experience to learn that the good news was for everyone, not only the chosen people.

Two features of violence are that it divides and it confuses. On the evening that the IRA ended its ceasefire on 9 February 1996 by bombing Canary Wharf in London, Brian was asked to take part in a TV panel discussion in Belfast. By the time he had driven up the motorway the voices on the radio were blaming the British government, the Irish government, the Churches, civil society and occasionally the IRA for the bomb. When a ceasefire breaks down all sides need to examine their conscience. Certainly at the time it seemed as if the British government was not seriously engaged in negotiations with the IRA. Nonetheless, it was the IRA's decision alone to plant and explode a lethal bomb. They decided to return to 'war' on behalf of the people of Ireland, without the consent of the people.

Reconciliation work, like violence, is also confusing. It cannot be done without entering into the world view of all the parties involved in the conflict. None of us succeed in this well enough. It is never a task that is complete, because there is always more to learn about other groups. At the same time one cannot lose one's own moral compass, and one has also to make judgements about what might help to reduce divisions. These judgements may often throw up tensions which can 'demagnetise' one's moral compass. Within this maze no one comes out perfect, so none of us can be self-righteous. That is a central Christian principle. We need to remind each other of it, and of the other Christian values of respect, compassion, understanding and justice. That is why it is so important for those who want to work for peace in divided societies to do so in groups that include members from all perspectives.

An example of this need for different perspectives occurred one day in Community Dialogue. About twenty people were sitting around the table. One person said that she had started to include the RUC (the police) in dialogue groups. A Republican immediately responded that if Community Dialogue engaged with the RUC he would leave. A Loyalist naturally came back with the statement that he would leave if the police were excluded.

Forty-five minutes later this issue was 'resolved'. 'Resolved' meant that enough wriggle room was found for people to stay together. There was no neat solution. The people involved were able to stay together only because they already had built a basis of respect and understanding which had been forged in the heat of deeply painful dialogues in which basic hurts and blames were expressed, and eventually heard. From that basis, somehow, enough glue was formed to enable us to stick together. That is an example of the importance of dialogue.

Chapter 13: Social Issues

A major problem with the legacy of the conflict in Northern Ireland is that it can distract us from focusing on social issues. Many of these are common not only to Northern Ireland and the Republic of Ireland but also to many European countries, and often need to be addressed at that level, as well as locally.

We have mentioned above that our Churches can be comfortable, often with better off people. Many get the message of charity and give to the poor. The message of Christ, however, was about justice as well as charity. There is a simple measurement for the humanity and justice of any society: how well it treats those with the least. This criterion applies in health, education, employment, wages and the environment. It is a criterion that is to be defended in general and on human grounds – the alternative is violent conflict – but it also expresses a value that was central to Christ, and must therefore be central to his followers too. Much of Christ's message on social issues had to do with following the values he had inherited as a part of the Jewish people: Amos's critique of corruption, written nearly 800 years before Christ, is shockingly contemporary:

> 'They hate the man who teaches justice at the city gate and detest anyone who declares the truth. For trampling on the poor man and for extorting levies on his wheat...I know how

many your crimes are and how outrageous your sins, your oppressors of the upright, who hold people to ransom and thrust the poor aside at the gates. That is why anyone prudent keeps silent now, since the time is evil' (*Am. 10-13*).

This does not tell us *how* to get justice. People will always rightly argue over ways to deliver it. The values of Christ do, however, give us values: we must privilege the marginalised. They also set parameters: if our policies leave people in poverty then we need to change them, and if we do not, we cannot be in relationship with God.

Homelessness

Most of those working in the area of homelessness in the Republic of Ireland reckoned that the situation in 2016 was as bad as they had ever known it. As well as the endemic causes such as depression, anxiety, addiction and other mental illnesses, rent prices had greatly increased over the previous few years. This meant that many new families joined the ranks of the homeless. This was one consequence of the fallout from the financial crisis that started in 2007–08. Having pushed easy money at people to encourage them to buy houses, often beyond their means, companies came looking for their pound of flesh when job losses led to an inability to meet loan repayments. This was one of many examples of a capitalism, not only with far too limited restraints, but without a moral compass. It was a startling illustration of what happens when the principle that money is an instrument to serve people is ignored.

By 2016 many financial institutions had recovered their losses, salaries had been maintained and bonuses were still being paid, but the effects of the crisis were still being felt by thousands paying mortgages with negative equity, and in many other ways.

Dealing with homelessness is complex. Solutions such as capping rents may have unexpected consequences. Other proposals, such as changing planning laws to allow building within the circle of the M50 in Dublin, a proposal put forward by economist Colm McCarthy, have not been discussed sufficiently. Certainly, the current solution of putting families in Bed and Breakfasts for long periods is not acceptable.

A huge increase in social housing is needed. This is going to cost money and there is no way to avoid this. The alternative is an increasingly divided society which is bad for everyone.

The high cost of housing is also an important disincentive to Irish people to come home. That is one reason why the Irish Health Service found it hard to fill nursing posts in 2015: the cost of living, including housing, was too high to persuade people who had emigrated to the UK, Australia and elsewhere to come back.

Homelessness is also a major issue in Northern Ireland. In 2013, 19,400 households were presented as homeless. Rates of statutory homelessness acceptances are higher in Northern Ireland than anywhere else in the UK (13.4 statutory acceptances per 1,000 households, as compared with 2.3 in England), partly as a result of policy and administrative practices that differ from those in Great Britain.[14]

As with many issues, a way forward depends on the priority given to it by the electorate. Politicians, for the most part, will do what they are told. If we want action on homelessness and housing it is up to people to demand this from their politicians.

Health

The same principle applies in health care. Health care costs will increase dramatically, both because of new medical treatments, and because of an aging population. This means Ireland is faced with stark choices: it can either follow the current trend of increasing private medical care and fail to respond to the need for increased care in the public sector, or it can do what some other countries in Europe and elsewhere do: provide much better medical care for all its people. There are stark choices here: do we want to provide optimum care for ourselves, or focus on developing a country-wide system that benefits the wider public? Do we want to prioritise the benefits to our own area by retaining a small local hospital, or follow best practice and support new centres of excellence, as, to be fair, the government seems to be doing? And, do we want to think of health care solely within national boundaries, or start looking for ways to maximise the use of facilities by different countries working together? Again, this is already happening to an extent.

Does the Republic of Ireland want to continue to give preference to those with private means or is it prepared to embark on the creation of a universal health system, like the NHS in the UK? In 1970 twenty per cent of people in the Republic had private health insurance. Now it is over fifty per cent. These are choices that we make. Different national groups choose to go in different directions: the UK, Canada, France, Germany and the Scandinavian countries have all chosen some form of universal health service. Some are better than others. But they all operate on the principle that sick people should to be treated because they are human beings and these countries are prepared to pay the price to fund this treatment. Other countries, such as the USA, go in a different direction. It seems to us that the solidarity practised by Christ points clearly towards health care for all.

Refugees
Many EU countries faced a huge influx of refugees in 2015. The sight of the dead body of three year old Alan Kurdi, drowned while his family attempted the dangerous crossing from Turkey to Greece, shows both the importance and limitations of communal emotion: undoubtedly the death of this child inspired many thousands across

Europe to take action on refugee issues, but how many others were deeply moved by Alan's death, yet would not have been willing to face the task of feeding, housing, educating and rearing him had he lived? Refugees are very much like other people: they need to eat, drink, learn, build houses, do business, keep healthy and celebrate their culture. The reason they are refugees is because they cannot do this in their own country, often for reasons linked to the actions of Western states.

The refugee crisis of 2015, which saw so many EU countries paralysed in their response, involved the largest movement of people in Europe since the Second World War, but it is likely to get much worse in future years: the wars that caused the crisis are on-going, so more and more parents are going to risk their own lives and those of their children by taking on the nightmare of crossing the Mediterranean. They will do this because the greater nightmare would be stay at home and face the daily and nightly barrage of bombs and bullets.

The refugee issue raises some tough questions: how many people can any one country take in? The answer is nearly always: more than we think. But this depends on the educational, skills, health and language capacity of the incomers. And, crucially, will the newcomers be able to live in peace with the religious and cultural values of the host country?

That question is of course a loaded one that needs unpacked: no culture stays the same and the host culture will be, and should be, changed by newcomers. There are, however, cases of cultural practices which cannot be accepted. Culture should never be accepted when it disrespects persons. Cultural pluralism is not a value desert. There may well be disagreement about where to draw the line on many issues, but there can be no ambivalence on issues of bodily integrity. Valid cultural challenges will not be one-way: just as Western culture will raise some questions for newcomers, so they too will raise questions about Western values.

It may be that there is an optimum percentage below which the number of refugees is not seen as a threat. So, for example, it is easy for host country residents to be nice to refugees when the refugees are less than five per cent of the population. It may be more difficult if, for example, the proportion rises to twenty-five per cent. But this in turn depends on other factors: are there already cultural or historical links between the two groups? Are the refugees competing for middle or working-class jobs and services?

There can be a class bias on refugee issues: some of the greater enthusiasts for their arrival are better-off people whose jobs, children's education and healthcare will not be affected. The vast majority of new arrivals in England are placed in poorer areas in the North, because housing is cheaper. This may save money in the short term, but it can also lay the foundations for costly social unrest in the long term.

Working class people can also create myths, which are then played on by populist politicians. A group of Loyalists with whom Brian worked were convinced that the 'brou' (welfare) gave new cars to all refugees, and that the refugees were bad devils: they had late night parties and got drunk – quite unlike the locals! Often people complain that 'they were taking our jobs' even though they themselves might sue anyone who offered them a job. These views, obviously, were not unique to Loyalists. They can be found in some sections of working class areas over Europe, just as more open views can also be found.

While the refugee issue is complex, some obvious points can be made: the number taken in by Western states (including Germany) is much smaller in percentage terms than countries like Lebanon and Jordan. In 2016 Lebanon had over 1 million (approximately twenty per cent of the population), Jordan had 629,000 (approximately eight per cent of the population).

Secondly, the issue is always a symptom of a problem. To reduce the symptom means dealing with the cause. That means bringing about peace in countries currently in conflict. There is no easy or obvious way to achieve this at the time of writing. The Syrian civil war seems intractable, a problem with no solution. This is exactly what people said about the Northern Ireland conflict, however, and problems here were 'solved', however imperfectly. There is no problem that *cannot* be solved. We cannot say how this will be done in Syria, but it seems obvious that part of the solution lies in the hands of international actors, perhaps especially Saudi Arabia and Iran. Western powers are deeply immersed in trade with the Saudis and could bring immense pressure to bear on them, if they chose to do so.

A third approach, which would certainly reduce deaths and terrible suffering, would be to process applicants in their home country, or in neighbouring countries that they have already reached, like Turkey.

Failing to respond strategically means that we approach the problem like people selling sticking plasters outside a factory in which faulty machines keep causing industrial accidents.

Refugees come for economic as well as safety issues. The answer to this is to change the balance of economic power between the host and refugee country.

There is a further issue that is already a major factor in the number of refugees, and it is likely to do so much more in the future: climate change. People will not stay in countries that are being drowned under water, or where the population is dying from drought. Climate change is going to lead to more and more of this, and this will lead to millions of new refugees.

There is a value question lying behind all these issues: how much do we cherish *solidarity*?

Chapter 14: Solidarity

It was startling to hear Irish Taoiseach Enda Kenny say in 2015, presumably as part of an election promise, that Ireland should follow the tax policy of the US. Does this mean that we should also take on its inequality? There is now a good deal of evidence to show that more equal societies do better on crime, health, education, and 'have much better chances of stronger and sustained economic growth'.[15]

This last point, about sustained economic growth, should surely be of interest to a country that has suffered so drastically from the tidal wave of the 2008 crash.

The key value in solidarity is that it balances the needs of the group and those of individuals, and it defines the group internationally as well as locally. *Balance* is important: it was, amongst other things, the failure of communism to recognise the importance of the individual that led to its demise. It was a similar failure that led unrestrained capitalism to collapse in 2007–08.

The issue of solidarity is dealt with directly by Jesus in the parable of the Rich Man and Lazarus (*Lk.16:19-31*). The rich man lived in great luxury, while Lazarus, who was covered with sores, had to be carried to the rich man's door in the hope of getting to 'eat the bits of food that fell from the rich man's table'. The nameless rich man goes to Hades, Lazarus to the bosom of Abraham. In his agony the rich man calls out to Abraham and asks him to send Lazarus to dip his finger in some water and cool his tongue, but Abraham responds: 'Remember, my son, that in your lifetime you were given all the good things, while Lazarus got all the bad things' and there is now a deep pit between the two which no one can cross.

In the story there is no indication that the rich man did anything wrong to Lazarus – he just did nothing. He probably did not even *see* him. How many times have we ourselves been struck by poverty when abroad, but fail to see it when we pass it every day at home? Our Lord is tough on this: if we want to connect to him, then we have to connect to our brothers and sisters in need. If we do not, then we separate ourselves from him. Homelessness, healthcare, refugees and other social issues become then a matter for eternal life.

For the Christian this should not be surprising. Our God is three. Our God is also one. We talk of God as three persons. But, since the Enlightenment, our idea of what a person is has changed: now a person is seen as a separate consciousness, an independent being, someone in some sense separate from and to an extent existing over and against other persons. God is not three persons in this sense. Yet, the Father is unique, the Son is unique and the Holy Spirit is unique. Each is distinct from the other. Yet, God is one.

This may sound like rarefied theology, but if we are Christian, whether we think about who God is or not, the implicit ideas we have about God influence our views of ourselves, of others and of society. Our God recognises each of us as unique. Yet, God calls us into relationship with each other. This is not simply an emotional relationship like that which led so many to recognise their connectedness with Alan Kurdi, but the thoughtful, committed type of relationship that will sit down with Alan's family and the wider community to work out how deaths like his can be avoided and how children like Alan can be fed and educated.

That is different from the view of God that sees him as someone in the clouds with whom I can have a loving relationship and who will look after me, irrespective of what happens to the rest of the world.

The European Community

The EU, as we remarked above, is one of the greatest conflict management instruments in history. It was an important player in the Northern Ireland peace process. When the UK and Ireland joined the EEC in 1973 they began a multilateral relationship with each other. This meant that government officials from both sides met on a variety of trade and other issues and built political relationships with each other. That meant that Northern Ireland was not the only issue, and this helped reduce tension to a degree. Further, other member states were able to ask the UK questions about what it was doing about the conflict. As well as this, the Republic found itself as an equal member among the eleven other member states, and this helped reduce feelings of inferiority and insecurity resulting from colonialism.

However, the European project is now under great strain. Much of this comes from right-wing parties reacting against Jihadist terrorism and the perceived threats of immigration. The financial crisis has also produced massive strains, almost leading to a Greek exit. Yet, that word 'almost' is important in the history of the EU. It is an institution that lives on the edge: it generally reaches agreement on important issues about five in the morning on the last night of negotiations. The EU is not a united state, so it has to resolve its differences continually through dialogue rather than by diktat. In this sense it may resemble the Anglican Communion more than the Roman Catholic Church. Yet, it has survived. The EU remains a mystery for many historians of institutions: prior to joining its members had no common language, religion, law or history. What many of its members had no common language, religion, law or history. What these members do have in common is a terrible history of war and the desire to build peace on interlocking economic systems. It also has outside countries still trying to enter it. It remains the best hope for human rights both for its residents, and for those of countries trying to join it, who are pressurised to act more justly. It has a capacity to introduce rights into member states that the states themselves would never do: the improvement in gay rights in Northern Ireland is one example.

This is not to suggest that the EU is without wrong. There will always be a battle between great business interests and the rights of workers. Corruption will always have to be opposed and bureaucracy challenged. Yet, it is difficult to see any way in which the great progress in rights and the improvement in living standards enjoyed by most – though not all – Europeans could have been achieved, absent the EU.

Brexit

Perhaps the greatest threat to the survival of the EU was the decision made by the people of the UK on 23 June 2016 to leave the union. Some of the criticisms of the EU made by the Leave side were justified: there is no felt connection between millions of EU citizens and European institutions; while migration and immigration benefits business, and will therefore help with some jobs, its greatest visible impact is likely to be felt in marginalised communities, especially in the north of England because that is where new immigrants are most likely to be dumped; it is quite understandable that large groups who have been left behind economically – for example in former mining areas – will want to give two fingers to obscenely rich people.

Other claims were not correct, to put it politely, including the much-publicised claim of the Leave campaign that £350 million would be saved by getting rid of the UK contribution to the

EU and that this would be invested in the NHS.

Also somewhat fanciful was the notion that sovereignty was being restored to the UK. In a globalised world sovereignty is often a fig leaf. It is particularly ironic that those who voted to leave to get greater sovereignty will now find themselves facing a potential veto from each one of the other twenty-seven EU countries if and when the UK seeks to extend the two years deadline which Article 50 imposes on any negotiations between the EU and a country that chooses to leave. This was graphically illustrated in 2016 when the Walloon parliament vetoed the EU–Canada free trade agreement, an agreement that took seven years to formulate. The reason the Walloons were able to do this was that they are one of the three federal regions in Belgium, and all have to agree on external treaties. In effect this means that if the UK fails to reach an agreement which satisfies twenty of the twenty-seven EU countries (a qualified majority) within two years of triggering Article 50, the Walloons, or any other individual country can veto any request to extend the negotiations. In that case failure to reach agreement simply leaves the UK with no trade agreement with the EU, and with no trade agreement with the World Trade Organisation (WTO). The economic impact of this will be very considerable, and will likely fall most on the poorer regions in which many voted for Brexit.

The Remain camp certainly did not make these issues clear enough during the referendum campaign.

It is obvious that there is a need to reform institutions. It is not obvious what the changes should be, or how to bring them about. Suggestions, such as holding a direct election process for the President of the European Commission, are positive. While desirable, however, this will not build a felt connection between voters and institutions. There is a need to give the electorate tangible benefits through linking with groups of similar interests in working class areas: for example on similar community based issues or trade union struggles.

Yet, these struggles need to be linked concretely to voting so that elections can be seen to make a difference. One of the key reasons why voting has declined in many Western countries is because people have made a rational decision that the outcome will make no difference to them. Absent a concrete connection between voting on the one hand and both people's day-to-day interests and their identity needs on the other, this will not change.

Migration was certainly a significant reason why many voted to leave the EU (it was also an important reason why many voted to stay). The fantasy was sold to many by Leave campaigners that it would be possible for the UK to restrict the free movement of people and still have tariff-free access to EU markets. This will not happen for the simple reason that if the EU concedes this for one country it will have to do so for all. The Remain camp pointed out quite validly that blaming migrants for the housing crisis was misplaced. The main reason for the shortage of houses was that not enough had been built. They also pointed to the huge number of immigrants working in the NHS and many service industries. The reason for this is that many UK workers lack the necessary qualifications, because of a lack of government investment.

The Remain camp failed to deal with the alienation of many white workers on the lower end of the economic scale. Financial globalisation has led to massive wealth for a relatively small number. There are certainly benefits for the general economy in this, for example in taxes. Yet, these benefits are too remote for the average worker. What they see is some people with huge wealth, and at the same time problems in their local areas with waiting times for places in hospitals and schools. The argument that health will always be a bottomless pit will make little impact, and the scapegoat chosen for the problems is not the government which cuts back on public services, nor the extremely wealthy who continue to support a financial system that breeds inequality, nor the multinationals who get massive benefits from tax avoidance. Instead people often blame migrants who in many cases are drawn to the UK both because they want to protect themselves from being killed, and also because there are jobs which they can do.

There is surely a lesson from the Brexit vote for the very rich: if they want to enjoy their wealth in a stable society they need to build solidarity with other groups in the country. Absent this the masses will destabilise the country.

The above issues cannot be dealt with by any country in isolation: that in the end is the crunch argument for the UK remaining a member of the EU. It can trade outside the EU while allowing free movement of people in return for access to EU markets while at the same time having no influence on EU regulations, or it can block free movement and pay tariffs, or it can remain a full member.

There was an initial economic response to Brexit: several major financial institutions started talking about their need to relocate in an EU country. Other investment firms blocked clients withdrawing funds in order to prevent a run on their assets. Financial markets around the work reacted negatively to the uncertainty and then stabilised, but the pound fell to its lowest level for over thirty years – something that will benefit UK exports but will negatively impact many other aspects of the economy. The falling exchange rate has a seriously negative impact on the amount of money received in Ethiopia by the charity Tim runs – another case of the poor being the first to suffer. In a few weeks sterling recovered and Brexit supporters argued that claims of negative impact were greatly exaggerated. But what happens in, say January 2019, two months before the end of negotiations with the EU if the British are still refusing to accept free movement of people, and the EU refuses to accept this? It is difficult to see how this will not lead to major economic pain.

Finally, of particular relevance to Northern Ireland, is the fact that both Northern Ireland and Scotland voted to remain. Each, like England and Wales, are countries of the United Kingdom. But it is the UK as such, and not its constituent countries, which has the power to enter or to leave the EU. There are legal constraints which may limit the capacity of the Westminster parliament to make decisions affecting both Scotland and Northern Ireland. The key word in that statement is 'may'. Neither of us is a lawyer, but it seems as if these constraints are matters of convention. How binding will they be? Our guess is that political decisions will dominate, with the use of some legal arguments to back them. In other words, if the more powerful group at Westminster decide that Brexit needs to be reversed they may use some ambiguity over the rights of Scotland and Northern Ireland to support this.

The Brexit vote has certainly led to an increased risk of a second Scottish independence referendum, but this is by no means certain. The UK government needs to approve a new referendum and this approval may not be forthcoming. Even if approval is given the Scottish National Party (SNP) may not opt for a referendum: politically it would be a disaster for them if they lost again. The fact that the Remain side in Scotland won on the EU issue does not mean that a majority would support the separate issue of leaving the UK: strong arguments will be put against the proposal, such as the question of a hard border with England, whether or not Scotland will need a separate currency, and whether the Scottish economy can sustain itself, especially in the light of falling oil prices. A further issue is whether Scotland would be admitted to the EU if it left the UK. The answer is not obvious. Several EU countries, perhaps most notably Spain, are under pressure from separatists. They are likely to oppose any options that reward the break-up of a state.

It is impossible to predict the future, but we are willing to bet that at some point before the end of the negotiations there will be growing calls for a second referendum. The reason for this seems obvious: just before the UK triggered Article 50, British Prime Minister Theresa May indicated that the UK would be pulling out of both the single market – in which goods, services, people and investments move freely – and the EU Customs Union – in which members share common tariffs. If the talks end up with the UK outside both there will certainly be major human and economic consequences. What these will be simply cannot be known in advance. Nor could it have been known when the UK voted on Brexit. It would therefore be entirely democratic to have a second referendum in which voters were asked if they still wanted to proceed with Brexit in the light of any agreement or lack of agreement at the end of negotiations. If the people have spoken once they can obviously speak a second time (or a third or fourth). That was the approach taken in the Republic of Ireland where it took two referenda to approve the Nice and Lisbon Treaties.

There is a key constitutional difference between the UK and Ireland: the UK is a parliamentary democracy, and Ireland is not. In the UK MPs elected by the people have ultimate power acting through parliament, not the people acting through referendum. The Brexit vote was not legally binding, unlike the referenda in Ireland. Yet, UK politicians from all sides said that they would 'respect the will of the people'. The UK constitution is unwritten: what constitutional impact, if any, will result from politicians – in parliament – speaking about the 'will of the people' as expressed in a referendum?

The immediate point, however, is that the Brexit referendum can be overturned in several ways: by a new referendum (which in itself, like the first, will have no legal power), by an election where candidates stand on a remain or a leave platform, or by an Act of Parliament.

Only parliament, unlike a new referendum or even a new election, has the constitutionally binding power to reverse the Brexit decision.

There is an interesting legal question about Article 50: once it is triggered by the UK, can the UK withdraw its application to leave within the two-year time frame for negotiations? This is not simply an academic point: when it becomes obvious that there will be no access to the single market without free movement, and further, when the economic cost of this becomes more visible, there is likely to be considerable 'buyer's regret'. So at that point could the UK suspend their application to leave?

Article 50 is silent on this point. So it seems as if the answer will be given either by a judge, or else by a political agreement with at least twenty of the EU states, or by some mixture of both. Suffice to say at this point that the general public are only slowly learning about the cost of Brexit.

The EU is obviously of vital importance to the Republic of Ireland. It is also important in the North. Nationalists in Northern Ireland often ignore UK issues: two weeks before the Brexit vote a local Sinn Fein activist asked Brian when the referendum was due to take place. The people of Ireland, North and South, voted in 1998 in favour of the proposition that Northern Ireland would remain part of the UK until the majority of the people in both the North and the South chose a United Ireland. It is perfectly legitimate for Nationalists to work for that outcome if they so choose. In the meantime, as citizens of the UK, they have a responsibility to work toward government policies that are respectful of others. The decision over Brexit will make a major impact for years to come. Nationalists need to be involved in this debate as much as anyone. . It was particularly regrettable that Sinn Fein, who won seven seats in the 2017 UK Westminster election, did not take their seats in parliament, which meant there were no Nationalists at Westminster. Had they done so they would not have given free rein to the DUP, with ten seats, to do a deal with the Tories that ensured a government majority.

If a hard border emerges as a result of Brexit it will have a huge negative impact on trade, and it will also have unpredictable political consequences.

Solidarity is a key value for Christians. Among other things this means that great disparities of wealth are not in keeping with Christ's Kingdom. Those who are very rich and want to be part of this kingdom need to address this issue. The poor are favoured by Christ, because they are poor.

We cannot jump from theological statements like these to claim Scriptural backing for either side of a political issue like Brexit. Nonetheless, it seems to us that solidarity is better achieved within the EU. It is difficult to see how there can be an effective opposition to unjust international systems such as that of untrammelled international finance other than through international cooperation. Certainly such cooperation can be developed in structures other than the EU. The EU, however, has been there in one form or another for over sixty years. It was and is the most effective conflict management structure in history: the wars between France and Germany in 1870, 1914 and 1939 and the lack of wars since 1945 are convincing evidence of this. It is an extraordinary example, with all its faults, of cooperation between countries with great differences of language, laws, culture and religion. It could be a basis for a much more positive structure that develops just trading relationships and solidarity both among its members and with other nations, especially Third World countries. This can only happen if the member states make it happen. Leaving the EU will do nothing to bring this about.

The election of Donald Trump as President of the USA was another symptom of the failure of solidarity. During his election campaign Trump called for a ban on all Muslims entering the US, building a wall with Mexico, undermining climate protection regulations, and described comments he made on tape in which he joked about sexual assault on women as 'locker room talk'. The fact that so many Americans voted for him shows the depth of alienation.

In several comments Trump made clear that he wanted to build a positive relationship with Vladimir Putin, that he supported Brexit, and that European countries should pay their fair share of the NATO budget instead of relying on the USA.

This raised obvious tensions with many EU countries some of which, at least at the time, were facing the possibility of further right wing electoral successes in the Netherlands and France. Most of these countries also supported sanctions against Russia because of its invasion of the Crimea and of Ukraine. Yet, ironically, Trump's comments about NATO may lead to a strengthening of the EU. Since the Second World war the EU has sheltered itself under the military umbrella of the USA. That was what protected it during the Cold War. In the new context US interests may focus more on the Pacific region than on Europe, and with isolationism seemingly growing more popular European countries may have tough choices to make about their defence budgets. They will face these in a context where health services in many European countries are under great strain. The withdrawal of the UK from the EU will make these issues all the more difficult, but the UK itself will face similar questions, and will do so in isolation, unless a deal is done.

The answer to the European crisis is not to back down on solidarity, or to dumb down respect for women, or for people from different religions or for immigrants. On the contrary, solidarity requires vigorously encouraging these. The way to do this is not by encouraging untrammelled capitalism which catches all workers in a downward spiral and in many areas greatly increases the pressures on local services. In a world where the liberal consensus of the past decades seems to have failed, there is a real need to seek a third way, which allows for free movement of people and capital, yet which also protects those who have been most hurt by them. The 'mixed economy' of the 1960s and 1970s may not have been such a bad thing after all.

Conclusion

Dreaming dreams

It is not easy to dream dreams in Northern Ireland. At least it is not easy to dream dreams that are not nightmares for others.

Given our focus on Christ and the way he lived, it is not surprising that our dreams are of peace, inclusion, overcoming poverty, finding ways to celebrate our differences and turning guns into ploughshares. However, dreams need to be turned into practical possibilities for living together. The stumbling along that we have achieved in Northern Ireland is infinitely better than the bombs and bullets of the past. But we humans can and should dream of more. Is it not time to make a fundamental revision of the 1998 Agreement and to set up a new devolved government in Northern Ireland without the sectarian requirement for all MLAs to designate themselves as 'Unionist', 'Nationalist' and 'Other'. Such a change seems like a pipe dream given that the major political parties would fear a loss of power from such a move. Our fear is that without this change they will maintain their power and continue to do so on a sectarian basis. Changing the way we designate our political leaders might in time lead to a change in reality, and then the sad divisions of the past – and present – might eventually fade as we move into a more human, and more Christian, future.

Does this stuff matter when life hurts? (Tim Kinahan)

At the end of this book we asked each other: do the issues raised in this book matter when life hurts?

Tim responded as follows:

Sometime during the writing of this book I suffered from writer's block, which enabled Brian to take over. Life hurt. All my energies were focused on processing the emotions involved in that hurt and I had little left for the intellectual or creative side of life.

A few years earlier my marriage had broken down and, although I had seemed at the time to 'cope with it well', I began to struggle down the line. Hence, the writer's block.

When I finally came clean to Brian as to the reasons for my silence he was, as is typical of him, extremely supportive. He asked one question, however, that I think needs to be asked – and that is the one that heads this section: *do the issues in this book matter when life hurts?* Are theological *minutiæ* important when life is on the rocks? Do the political and social implications of that theology have any relevance when personal life is unravelling? Does it matter what the Church and politicians do when all we need is a bit of balm to soothe our wounds?

Those are not straightforward questions and the answers, insofar as they exist, are not straightforward either. I have often maintained that, in many ways, questions are more important than answers – and indeed this book has far more questions than answers – but was it not true, when I was in the slough of despondency, that what I needed above all else was answers?

On a superficial level, yes, these things do matter as they form the context in which we live our personal and social lives. A strong society is a better place to live and to process our own personal issues; a society that 'works' is one that is going to be a more amenable place in which to thrive. The more dysfunction there is in the world around us, the more that is likely to infect our own personal dysfunction.

But that is, as I have said, superficial. Brian's question actually pulled me out of the self-pitying place in which I was beginning to get destructively comfortable. The questions with which this book wrestles have engaged me for much of my adult life. They have motivated me, inspired me, and given me purpose. By wallowing in my own personal problems I was actually smothering a lot of what has made me tick for the last forty years. By wallowing I was denying a fundamental part of who I am and thus actually compounding my problems.

In a sense it did not matter what those issues were. They could have been about the environment or concerns with international development: what mattered was that I had something to grapple with, something to engage me. The *process* was what, to some degree, made me live. I needed to re-engage with that, to re-engage with the issues, and thereby to re-engage with myself. The process was the answer, even if it never produced 'answers'.

That is a very personal perspective which does not answer the wider issue of whether what we have been grappling with in these pages is relevant in a world in which there seem to be far more pressing issues – modern day slavery, poverty, alienation, starvation and the rise of Jihadist extremism to name but a few. We believe that the issues we have addressed are important, and not just because they are 'our' issues.

In Ireland today we live in a society that has been indelibly influenced by Christianity, particularly in its Protestant and Roman Catholic manifestations. Many are now rebelling against this, for understandable reasons, and would like to deny this past. However, real and successful denial is not possible as the Christian world-view has moulded this land more deeply than even a few generations can erase. Many of the things that are good about this island and its values have their origins in Christian thinking and praxis. Much of what is bad also has its origins in Christianity – or, we would argue, in mistaken out-workings of the faith.

Although our Churches are not nearly as influential as they once were (and that is mostly a good thing) they still have a role to play in society. Our Churches, and their teaching, are still important to a significant minority of people in this island and therefore it is very important that our Churches think critically about who they are and how they want to influence society as a whole. The way Christians and the Churches more generally think moulds what they say and how they behave. Therefore it is very important that we go back into the habits of thought that shape who we are: get that right and we reflect Christ; get it wrong and we have seen all too clearly where that has led us. Ultimately, society is more important than our own individual pain.

So these issues are important. They are important because they contribute to the debate about the sort of society we want to create here in twentieth century Ireland, a society that reflects what is good in our history, but also challenges what has been awry. We believe that our history is important, but we also realise that much within it has been very negative. Denying this can only be illusory and create something without foundations. Our history, our foundations, need critical examination if we are to build on them properly. We hope that this book contributes positively to that debate.

Is Christ important today? (Brian Lennon)

Clearly, both of us think the answer to this question is yes, and Tim has written movingly above about the significance of Christ to him when he was going through a particularly difficult time. There are apparently good reasons, however, as to why so many answer this question negatively or agnostically.

Gone are the days when people believed in God simply because they feared hell. Yet, this has made it easy to see God as the bland irrelevance we outlined in our first chapter. Certainly, if God and Christ are bland, they do not exist. One source of the temptation to see God as irrelevant comes from a good, not a bad source: the new found respect between Churches and religions, and the willingness of people of faith to listen with humility to secularists. This is based on the valuable insight that God is at work not only in individuals but also in groups of people, and therefore in Churches and faiths other than our own. A second source of temptation is the equally positive insight that what matters most in faith is how we treat other people. It will be primarily on this that the Lord will question us when we meet him in the next life (*Mt.25:31-46*).

Both these insights make it easy to fall into the trap of thinking that it is not vital whether or not we believe in God, in Christ, the Eucharist, the church, the sacraments or the many other things that each of us see as highly important.

A third temptation is to conclude that theological issues are too difficult. Who knows the answers? If there is a God, God will be kind to us. So let's forget about difficult questions about life, death and the hereafter, and live our lives here and now as best as we can.

The Catholic theologian, Raymond Brown, gives a good answer to these questions when discussing the humanity and divinity of Christ.[16] Does it matter if Christ is one with God, or if he is really not God at all, but merely human, or if he is not human at all, but only God? Are not these questions best left in the fourth and fifth centuries, when Christians really debated them?

Brown responds that these issues matter a lot. If Christ is not really human, then God has not fully entered our world, God is really outside our world and can have no real understanding of what it is to be human. But if Christ is fully human, and also fully divine, then our God cannot live without us. Further, we have in Christ an image of what it is to be fully human, fully alive. We have a calling to live life to the full, to recognise that God's community is breaking into our world, and to celebrate the hope that this brings. Clearly we also are called to do whatever we can to change the suffering of our brothers and sisters, who are also the brothers and sisters of Christ.

For myself, I have experienced Christ's absence often at times when life was most difficult for me, difficulties often caused primarily by myself. But in looking back on these periods I could see ways in which Our Lord was present, drawing me out of whatever mess I had got into, but primarily doing this through other people. Sometimes this was through others who challenged me, sometimes through close friends (often the ones who challenged me). Looking back – and looking back like this is something Ignatius encourages in the *Spiritual Exercises* – helped me come to the belief that Christ will never give up on any of us, and in the end is incapable of letting go of any of us in any final sense.

That relationship with Christ has also enabled me to see that death is not an end of relationships, but a changing of them, and it has given me a belief that our relationships in this life are not temporary phenomena, but part of our initiation into the dance of the Trinity.

Our relationships are not only with those we know personally. Our God is immersed in *all* the people on the planet, and the community that Christ came to bring about is breaking into the world. As our knowledge of our universe expands, as we realise more and more that the rock we inhabit is but one of billions in the universe, it seems even more outlandish to believe that at the centre of everything is one human being who lived a short life in a remote part of a small country. Yet, that is the nature of our God: at once universal, and intimately local.

Because God is universal Christians are called not only to an intense personal relationship with Christ, but also to be God's eyes and mouth, God's hands and feet, in building the community of peace, of respect and of justice that God is bringing about.

Many years ago my mother chose the following piece, written by Clement of Alexandria, for the memorial card for my uncle, a Jesuit who served as a chaplain in World War II, and then lived the remainder of his life in Australia:

> 'You will join the dance of the angels
> As they circle the God who knows no death…
> And by my grace, you, too,
> Will know no death.
> I endow you with my mind,
> Which is the knowledge of God,
> And with my whole self.
> This is what I am about;
> This is what God wants;
> This is the music and harmony
> Composed by the Father.'

Dancing in the circle of the one God – who is Three Persons – with all others in the world is, in the end, what life is about.

(Endnotes)

1 An Inter-Church Group on Faith and Politics, *Breaking Down The Enmity*, Section Two, (Dublin: *Studies*, 1984).

2 A locally-raised regiment of the British army.

3 http://www.timothyarcher.com/kitchen/the-table-of-the-lord-old-testament-meals/.

4 There are dangers in any language that we use about God. The meaning of 'persons' has changed over the centuries, and a widespread understanding today of the term today as separate conscious beings in opposition to each other does not meet the nuances of Trinitarian dogma. But nor does seeing God only as a single person.

5 17 October 2015, to a gathering of bishops, http://voiceofthefamily.com/papal-call-for-decentralization-puts-integrity-of-catholic-doctrine-at-risk/.

6 *The Irish Times*, 16 September 2014.

7 Raymond Brown, *The Churches the Apostles Left Behind*, (London: Cassell, 1984), p.43, footnote 61.

8 Seamus Heaney, The Biretta, from *Seeing Things* (1991).

9 Derek Mahon, 'Ecclesiastes', from his *Collected Poems* (1999).

10 'Declaration on Certain Questions Concerning Sexual Ethics' of December 29, 1975, n.8, par 4, noted in the same congregation's Letter to the Bishops of the Catholic Church on the Pastoral Care of Homosexual Persons (par 3), 1 October 1986. https://www.belfastinterfaceproject.org/interfaces-map-and-database-overview.

11 Available from Messenger Publications www.messenger.ie

12 https://www.belfastinterfaceproject.org/interfaces-map-and-database-overview. 12

13 This is the title of a chapter in Brian's book, *Peace Comes Dropping Slow*, (Belfast: Community Dialogue, 2004).

14 Suzanne Fitzpatrick, Hal Pawson, Glen Bramley, Steve Wilcox and Beth Watts, (Northern Ireland: Crisis, *The Homelessness Monitor*, 2013).

15 Nat O'Connor, Research Director of TASK and one of the authors of *Cherishing all Equally*, a report issued in February 2015.

16 *Jesus God and Man*, (New York: Macmillan, 1967).